CCCC STUDIES IN WRITING

Edited by Victor Villanueva, W

The aim of the CCCC Studies in Writing & Rhetoric Series is to influence how we think about language in action and especially how writing gets taught at the college level. The methods of studies vary from the critical to historical to linguistic to ethnographic, and their authors draw on work in various fields that inform composition—including rhetoric, communication, education, discourse analysis, psychology, cultural studies, and literature. Their focuses are similarly diverse—ranging from individual writers and teachers, to work on classrooms and communities and curricula, to analyses of the social, political, and material contexts of writing and its teaching.

SWR was one of the first scholarly book series to focus on the teaching of writing. It was established in 1980 by the Conference on College Composition and Communication (CCCC) in order to promote research in the emerging field of writing studies. As our field has grown, the research sponsored by SWR has continued to articulate the commitment of CCCC to supporting the work of writing teachers as reflective practitioners and intellectuals.

We are eager to identify influential work in writing and rhetoric as it emerges. We thus ask authors to send us project proposals that clearly situate their work in the field and show how they aim to redirect our ongoing conversations about writing and its teaching. Proposals should include an overview of the project, a brief annotated table of contents, and a sample chapter. They should not exceed 10,000 words.

To submit a proposal, please register as an author at www.editorial manager.com/nctebp. Once registered, follow the steps to submit a proposal (be sure to choose SWR Book Proposal from the drop-down list of article submission types).

THE DESIRE FOR LITERACY
WRITING IN THE LIVES OF ADULT LEARNERS

Lauren Rosenberg
Eastern Connecticut State University

Conference on College Composition and Communication

National Council of Teachers of English

Staff Editor: Bonny Graham
Series Editor: Victor Villanueva
Interior Design: Mary Rohrer
Cover Design: Mary Rohrer and Lynn Weckhorst
Text Images: Jon Crispin

NCTE Stock Number: 10812; eStock Number: 10829
ISBN 978-0-8141-1081-2; eISBN 978-0-8141-1082-9

It is the policy of NCTE in its journals and other publications to provide a forum for the open discussion of ideas concerning the content and the teaching of English and the language arts. Publicity accorded to any particular point of view does not imply endorsement by the Executive Committee, the Board of Directors, or the membership at large, except in announcements of policy, where such endorsement is clearly specified.

Every effort has been made to provide current URLs and email addresses, but because of the rapidly changing nature of the Web, some sites and addresses may no longer be accessible.

Publication partially funded by a subvention grant from the Conference on College Composition and Communication of the National Council of Teachers of English.

Library of Congress Cataloging-in-Publication Data
Rosenberg, Lauren, 1963-
    The desire for literacy : writing in the lives of adult learners/Lauren Rosenberg, Eastern Connecticut State University.
        pages cm. — (CCCC studies in writing & rhetoric)
    Includes bibliographical references and index.
    ISBN 978-0-8141-1081-2 ((pbk))
    1. Reading (Adult education) 2. Literacy. I. Title.
    LC5225.R4R65 2015
    374'.0124—dc23
                                                            2015007203

For Bob
and
for Bess and Ella
who nourish me daily simply by being

CONTENTS

ACKNOWLEDGMENTS

I begin these pages with some sadness because the people I am most indebted to—the four participants whose stories and writing are the center of this book—must remain masked by pseudonyms. I want to whisper their names at least so they can know how deeply their words have resonated with me for more than ten years since I first met them. I understand how the Institutional Review Board protects them, protects me, protects institutions; and yet, even now I cannot fully express my appreciation. So I open by keeping them in disguise, the four participants who *are* this book, and I try to slip my voice behind their masks. To Violeta, Chief, George, and Lee Ann: my utmost admiration and gratitude.

The four participant-authors were not the only ones who shared their stories with me. I am thankful for the larger view, the background, history, and context that I gained from the staff at the Read/Write/Now Adult Learning Center and from the other literacy workers with whom I've consulted over the years. When I connected with the project manager at Read/Write/Now, I had found the place for my research. The teachers and project manager, Melissa, Carolyn, and Pamela (also pseudonyms), have been wonderful resources. They became important teachers to me as I watched them model how adult literacy education looks on the ground.

Lynne Weintraub, coordinator of the ESL Center at the Jones Library in Amherst, Massachusetts, was my first contact in the community of literacy workers in western Mass, and she introduced me to everyone else. Inson Chagnon taught me about many of the conflicts facing adult literacy learners. Marilyn Gillespie (when I finally did meet her) filled in the blank spaces and enriched my perspective.

Like many academic first books, this one has its roots in a dissertation. I remain inspired by the wisdom of my original committee members at the University of Massachusetts Amherst: Donna LeCourt, Anne Herrington, and Gretchen Rossman, fine scholars who showed me how to do it.

At Eastern Connecticut State University, I received funding from six years of Connecticut State University American Association of University Professors research grants directed toward this project. My colleagues at Eastern make my days full and lively. I am thankful to those I laugh and gossip with, especially Reginald Flood, Rita Malenczyk, and Maureen McDonnell. Most of all, my smart, curious, nonjaded students make my academic work meaningful. Their commitment to asking the hard questions keeps me questioning too.

Eli Goldblatt was the first person to take this book project seriously in a way that I couldn't have expected and had to learn to trust. At our initial meeting (at a small table in the back of the Exhibit Hall at the CCCC Annual Convention in St. Louis), I demanded of him: Why do you want to help me? What's in this for you? At the time, I truly could not fathom why someone would reach out the way he did—rejecting an early proposal and then encouraging me—without another motivation. By now I have come to understand that his commitment to our field and to supporting new voices joining the conversation is genuine. Eli's kind of investment is rare.

Donna LeCourt has been an extraordinary friend for many years, crossing boundaries from professor and mentor, to close friend, and recently to manuscript reader. From Donna I have learned that friendship can extend in many directions, and that each of the directions has its moment and purpose. We remind each other that our hard work is balanced with lightness: sometimes we are unpacking the challenges of our institutional lives; sometimes we are swimming in the ocean.

Donna and Anna Rita Napoleone have been the most excellent readers of this book in progress. I could not ask for a better writing group or more honest readers to question me and to remind me of how other readers might read and respond, what their own students might say, what their family members might say, how all of these ways of reading and understanding are vital to consider. I am grateful for such friends who are also critical and caring readers.

Victor Villanueva, my Studies in Writing & Rhetoric series editor, guided me on the long journey to publication with kindness and truthfulness. From the moment we began work together, he insisted, "I want folks to meet these folks." Our conversations (in writing and face to face) about the specifics of the project, and also about stories and theory and the state of our profession, encouraged my continual interrogation of my purposes. Victor's openness and willingness to devote enormous amounts of time to working with me on shaping the book, taking seriously all of my questions and always responding immediately and honestly, have changed me as a writer. His fierce support gave me the courage to write this book this way.

Thanks to Bonny Graham at NCTE for editing the book with respectful attention, precision, and humor, and for reinvigorating my analysis right at the end of the project. I am grateful as well for permission to use Jon Crispin's photographs of learners at Read/Write/Now.

Many friends shared my writing experiences over hikes deep in the woods, cups of coffee, lunches and dinners, glasses of wine, barking dogs, and always so much talk. I am blessed to have wonderful friends from near and far (and the far ones do seem near): Maria Black, Mike Edwards, Collie Fulford, Emma Howes, Mari L'Esperance, Karen Miscall-Bannon, Margaret Price, Michelle Santangelo, Diane Schwemm, Sarah Spieldenner; along with the other guides: Joyce Braunhut, Davina Miller, and Patty Townsend. Thank you for listening.

Having been raised in a storytelling tradition, I learned to value the crafting of narrative at a young age. Starting with my grandmother's opener, "Listen! I'm telling you so you'll know," I was fed a rich broth of stories, of who did what to whom and for what gain, and so on. I am appreciative of my family, who sustain this interest in performing our stories and studying the words of others: my parents and sister, Ellen, Jerry, and Liz Rosenberg. Thanks to my in-laws, Anne and Charlie Hepner, for their ongoing support.

Finally, to my closest people, my husband and daughters, the dedication is just a gesture. You have done the real work of living through this project with me in all its incarnations. You remind me when it's time to talk about it, when you have had enough, and when it is time to rest and love.

A note about the contents of this book. Some of the material from the participants has appeared in other venues; however, the arguments and analysis are new to the book. An article on Violeta's gestures toward textual agency was published in "'You Have to Knock at the Door for the Door Get Open': Alternative Literacy Narratives and the Development of Textual Agency in Writing by Newly Literate Adults," *Community Literacy Journal* (2008). George's examination of his experiences with literacy and nonliteracy appeared in "Retelling Culture through the Construction of Alternative Literacy Narratives: A Study of Adults Acquiring New Literacies," *Reflections: Writing, Community Literacy, and Service Learning* (2010).

1

Resisting Nonliteracy: Adult Learners Restory Their Narratives

GEORGE, A SIXTY-YEAR-OLD AFRICAN AMERICAN man who has been learning to read and write during the last few years, recalls an interaction he had with a nonliterate woman while waiting in the cashier's line at the supermarket:

> I think it was the store somewhere, and um, the person was ahead of me. She didn't know what she was doing because— see this big sign right there? But it's just like I say: You don't know how to read and write; . . . you don't know what that sign up there saying. And I was able to assist [her], to show her. I didn't do it in a way to make myself look big, doing the way to try to embarrass her 'cause of other peoples behind me. . . . I put it in a way, like, "Well, you just didn't see that, didn't see that word." But I know she saw that word; she didn't know what it is. You don't do it [help someone read] to try to harm someone else, make yourself look big; . . . you do something to try to help somebody . . . in a way that you won't embarrass the person; you know what I mean? . . . 'Cause you got to look at the time when, when you couldn't read or write. I look at it myself . . . somebody had embarrassed me too. Oh yeah, I been embarrassed. It got to the point: "Well, can't you read?" And do you know? I can't. [*laughs*] . . . "You can't read!"

This is George now, proud that he is literate and able to help someone else in the way he would like to have been helped himself, telling yet another story about a time he spent at the store and what goes on there. He loves going to the supermarket and walking the aisles, and he loves reading the labels on things.

George's memory of intervening in a nonliterate woman's shopping experience to prevent a painful encounter exemplifies the kind of restorying that the four adults in this book engage in as they become more literate. Here, he expresses his awareness of how nonliteracy operates. Now that he is able to read and write, George has the confidence to flip the incident into a narrative in which he can be compassionate and act on someone else's behalf.

His display of sensitivity and action also reveals a benefit I gained from working with him. Testimonies like George's helped me, a researcher studying people's experiences of acquiring new literacies, understand why and how people claim literacy for their own purposes. I learned from George and his peers to read carefully between and underneath the layers of stories like this one to look for multiple expressions of how people respond to the ways literacy is used to manipulate and denigrate, as well as to look for what motivates individuals to confront the subject position of "illiterate."[1] Over the years of my study, and afterwards when I extended my work into a longitudinal project with two of the original participants, I found that adult learners already possess critical awareness of how an ideology of literacy has positioned them as less than whole. I also learned through this project that their motivation to seek literacy later in life comes from a long-term desire to read and write that is not necessarily linked to material or ideological aspirations.

This book is the result of a qualitative study of the motivations and writing practices of adults who pursued literacy education by their own choice. Though the project began as an investigation into the reasons people might have for becoming literate, my focus on a few adults' experiences led me—along with them—to look more widely at the roles literacy has played throughout their lives and into older adulthood when, as people who are no longer active in the workforce, they now choose to study.[2] I discovered that the four participants pursue literacy despite material conditions that have repeatedly reminded them that literacy is not for them. Their stubbornness, resilience, and continued desire to right something in their lives intrigued me as I observed students at the Read/Write/ Now Adult Learning Center and eventually settled on the learners who are the subjects of this book.

They go to a learning center situated in an urban public library in Springfield, Massachusetts, a location that is easy enough to get to by bus or car, but a place apart from their prior lives, which contained little print text. The participants provide compelling narratives, yet their stories carry more significance than simply conveying how they dealt with hardship and confronted adversity through literacy education. Their unrelenting wish to become more literate over the course of their lives suggests that the desire for literacy is intrinsic, transcending other, more obvious motivations, such as economic and personal improvement. The accounts of nonliterate Americans tend to go unheard in the mostly literate mainstream because this population is rendered voiceless by a society that equates education with cognitive ability.

To this extent, nonliterate Americans satisfy Gayatri Chakravorty Spivak's definition of a *subaltern class,* that sector of the population whose experience counters the dominant and who are, therefore, shut out from dominant ideological concerns. Spivak asks, "Are those who act and *struggle* mute, as opposed to those who act and *speak* . . . ?" (275). Her question,[3] though originally directed at postmodern intellectuals, asks most importantly: Who has the right to speak? Can those people whom hegemonic culture has positioned as voiceless find a space to resist their positioning and speak out?

The common presumption that a person who can't read is a person who can't know invalidates the experiences of some Americans and denies that they have critical perspective. Just because a person doesn't know how to read or write doesn't mean that person is unable to think. Mike Rose has argued that "to be literate is to be honorable and intelligent. Tag some group illiterate, and you've gone beyond letters; you've judged their morals and their minds" ("Language" 354). This judgment is at the root of the embarrassment George speaks of, which he will go out of his way to help another person avoid. In his account of how the woman in the supermarket was treated, he acts to maintain her dignity. Yet, while he may be motivated primarily by an impulse to protect her from being insulted by the condescending behaviors of more literate cashiers and customers, George also knows from his own experience that even though some people might be unconscious in their judgment of others, at times people are deliberately demeaning and will purposely hurt others by insulting their abilities.

ACCEPTING AND RESISTING DOMINANT DISCOURSES OF LITERACY

When adult learners come to literacy centers, they express their experiences in terms of scripts that have positioned them as "illiterate," a label they have applied to themselves. Wendy Hesford uses the term *autobiographical scripts* to name the narratives projected onto people by institutions, culture, and ideology, "the culturally available models of identity and narrative templates that surround experiential history" (xxi). Dominating discourses do not exist solely in culture outside of ourselves; we also embody them. As Frantz Fanon observes, the colonized individual internalizes the way culture has been imposed on him as he "passes from psychological dependence to psychological inferiority" (*Black Skin* 98). External agents and institutions, such as schools, employers, and church, then reinforce our scripts. In Louis Althusser's terms, these institutions and organizations inscribe the ideology of the State upon its subjects (128). For example, both George and one of his peers, Lee Ann, speak of themselves as a "dummy" when they reflect on how they were gazed upon in school. When we tell our stories, we (all of us) perform our autobiographical scripts. Experience cannot be expressed outside of socially dictated scripts unless individuals consciously work to construct their autobiographical scripts differently.

Marilyn Gillespie, a researcher in adult basic education and the founder of the center where this study is based, observed that people who attend literacy programs typically express the wish for acceptance into dominant culture. Learners believe that literacy will offer them the agency they have been denied, when actually the power they seek is not tied to literacy itself but to cultural benefits afforded to many of those who are already literate. Gillespie notes that "for many [newly literate] authors literacy seemed to have come to stand for knowledge itself. To be illiterate was to be without knowledge, opinions, or voice" ("Becoming Authors" 149). But I found that even nonliterate people know there is more to power and social injustice than the written word. George dances around this presumption when he shields a nonliterate woman from an attack on her dignity, using his own literacy to keep her from being targeted.

In spite of his restorying, George, like all of the people I studied, is concerned with accommodation as well as resistance. Part of his drive to become literate is about fitting into a dominant culture of literacy that has excluded him. Finding a place is not simple; there is an unclear line between assimilating practices because they might give people a different role in the social order and opposing practices because people are keenly aware of how those practices have been used against them. As outsiders to the literate mainstream, nonliterates want acceptance; yet they also criticize, resist, and sometimes seek to change an unjust system. Their efforts to strike a balance between accommodation of and resistance to dominant discourses as they become more literate were a compelling feature of the participants' spoken and written stories, and ones that I examine in these chapters.

In looking at George as someone who shuttles between accommodation and resistance, I find it useful to think through Geoffrey Chase's explanation of accommodation, opposition, and resistance. Opposition, according to Chase (informed by Henry Giroux's resistance theory) moves against the dominant, but it isn't *toward* anything. It remains attached to dominant ideology, in contrast to the disruption that accompanies resistance. Chase's terms help illustrate the concepts that are so important in Antonio Gramsci's work, particularly how opposition maintains hegemony whereas resistance has a counterhegemonic "revealing function" (Giroux qtd. in Chase 20); this is what Chase calls the "sustained refusal [that] constitutes resistance" (21). Opposition is still tied to hegemonic practices, while resistance reaches toward something else, opposing or contradicting with the intent to change. Throughout this book, I examine incidents when adult learners exhibited the "sustained refusal" of resistance. I see such moments as expressions of a turbulent flow that I associate with naming and reacting to conflicting discourses.

Competing pressures to accommodate and resist reflect the contradictions people struggle with as subjects of and to ideology; in the case of adult learners, their experiences cause these oppositions to collide in a turbulent flow. Collisions of discourses create turbulence as people navigate their everyday experiences. In fluid dynamics, *turbulent flow* names an irregular or chaotic movement that causes ongoing, persistent mixing rather than linear or predictable patterns. Turbulent flow is the effect of disruption in moving bodies; it arises naturally yet is necessarily tumultuous. Dominant and alternative discourses are always mixing in adult learners' experiences of relating to literacy and cannot be separated out.

Most of the time, however, in their daily conversations, the participants in this study express their desire for literacy as Gillespie ("Becoming Authors") describes it, in terms of dominant ideology, with the hope that education will undo "illiteracy." They convey a dominant assumption of nonliteracy as a pathology that causes social problems, and of the nonliterate individual as a person who should be treated with remediation, rather than considering nonliteracy as symptomatic of a society that places blame for its problems on certain citizens.[4] According to critical educators Giroux (*Border Crossings,* "Literacy"), Peter McLaren, and Ira Shor, the problem of dominant ideologies is that they do not encourage people to critically interrogate culture. If adult learners were simply to accept dominant ideologies concerning literacy unquestioningly, they would reproduce the very system that constructed them as "illiterate" and go on to subjectify others, thus reinforcing rather than altering their autobiographical scripts.

But the desire to become more literate is often fraught with equally strong competing impulses to quit, to denigrate oneself, to change one's mind, to remain grounded in work for wages rather than permitting oneself to value studying. Affective reasons for be-

coming literate are even more turbulent than the social and material forces we have come to expect. In their struggle to cope with
competing discourses, adult literacy learners sometimes respond in
provocative, unpredictable ways that reveal their refusal to comply.
The spaces of resistance they create suggest the possibility for coun-
terhegemony within a turbulent flow.

The idea that adult learners might disrupt patterns of accommodation to change their autobiographical scripts may seem out of
reach for learners at a literacy center, but that is precisely what the
participants in this study did. When the four people talked about
their literacy histories, and even more so when they restoried their
experiences in writing, they transcended dominant discourses by
expressing alternative reasons for pursuing literacy. They did this
because their experience continually places them in opposition to
the mainstream, which is not necessarily a position they choose.
But as people who *have* deliberately chosen their literacy education
(sometimes at emotional and social risk), they do have convictions
about their decision to study.

They also at times doubt the culture that has marginalized them.
I see both contradiction and irony in the possibility that people

who are acquiring new literacies might exercise agency over aspects of their lives in which they have been oppressed. In Spivak's terms, the question is whether the subaltern has the ability to critique her position, which has little agency. Since nonliterate people have been rendered without voice, knowing how and when to speak for themselves (and with what language) is necessarily challenging. Spivak argues, "For the 'true' subaltern group, whose identity is its difference, there is no unrepresentable subaltern subject that can know and speak itself" (285). The subaltern is limited by her social position, which restricts her ability to speak.

But I have seen that when people do get the space to speak out by constructing narratives counter to those that have been scripted for them, they sometimes want to express a complex critique of how culture operates and how they have been positioned. Through their newly acquired literacy, adult learners become able to voice their analysis in previously unavailable ways.

Their experience on the margins puts people in a position where they, more than many, are willing to question dominant views. At bottom, underneath the predictable moral and economic reasons for becoming more literate, is something else: desire rooted in an affectual motivation to read and write. For two of the participants in the study, Violeta and Chief, the ability to claim text as their own—to have textual agency—and to use it for social action is at the heart of their motivation to become more literate. The potential to act and express themselves differently matters more than what they might gain materially. The other two, Lee Ann and George, reach toward new relationships with writing, yet the act of writing remains daunting and is often a source of frustration. They resist dominating perspectives primarily through their oral critique, by articulating a counternarrative.

The counternarratives people express result from their affectual experiences. Sara Ahmed offers a perspective not unlike Fanon's about the effects of power on individual and social identity. Informed by feminist and queer scholars, she examines how "emotions can attach us to the very conditions of our subordination" (12). In Ahmed's view, affect is itself a form of capital that resides neither solely within individuals nor with society but rather with both simultaneously. Affect comes from society in toward the individual and from the individual outward, reflecting the power relations that shape society and that also create the concept of Other. Our individual emotions reflect the way power has been acted upon us. This gives us the turbulent flow that we see performed as the result of people's embodiment of their experience, including their desire for literacy.

In the stories that the four participants I focus on tell about their literacy histories, they usually voice dominant views of education, economics, and moral self-improvement. They talk about becoming a "better" person through literacy, but what "better" means varies from person to person and reflects these overlapping discourses. Literacy offers the possibility to become more "independent" (Lee Ann); to "depend about myself" (Violeta); to become "self-sufficient" (George); to "better myself" (Chief). This idea of an improved individual suggests that becoming a better person depends on self-care that one accesses through education. Michel Foucault states that within a society, individuals will take it upon themselves to construct an acceptable subject that fits in with the dominant moral code ("Ethic" 14–15); and Donna LeCourt explains how "the goal of this care [of self] has shifted. Rather than seeking to attain freedom through transforming oneself into a moral subject, the individual believes the route to freedom is through transforming herself into a *knowing* subject" (*Identity Matters* 91–92, emphasis added). Education has become the currency with which a person improves to become a better subject of culture.

LOCATING THE ANALYSIS IN NARRATIVE

Literacy scholars may know already that people sometimes want literacy for alternative purposes, but we haven't yet examined the actual narratives people create as counterhegemonic gestures. Spivak points to people in the "margins (one can just as well say the silent, silenced center) of the circuit marked out by this epistemic violence, men and women among the illiterate peasantry, the tribals, the lowest strata of the urban proletariat" (283), as those whose experience must be represented differently—by them and according to their own view of their conditions. The parentheses in this statement are crucial: the subaltern position is not adequately represented, except perhaps in a utopian way, as hope for a more literate future. Spivak's question of whether the subaltern can speak points to problems of representation both from the outside and from within.

Concern over representation of marginalized people spurs Spivak's essay; her worry (derived from Gramsci) is with "the intellectual's role in the subaltern's cultural and political movement into the hegemony" (283), a well-intentioned role but one that further essentializes the Other because professional critics tend not to recognize their own subjectivity as influencing their construction of the subaltern. I am aware that I too, as a literacy researcher foregrounding the experiences of a vulnerable population, run the risk of essentializing because of my own conflicting roles as a first-culture person who can both disable and enable the people in this book from speaking. Yet I have tried to be mindful of my own position and not assume its "transparency" and to take responsibility for the work of presenting other people's words, as Spivak insists: "The subaltern cannot speak. . . . Representation has not withered away. The female intellectual as intellectual has a circumscribed task which she must not disown with a flourish" (308). Because I come from the outside and am now publishing other people's stories, I always risk speaking for them. However, the four people in this book are not simply subject to my representation. Their narratives create a performance of self-representation. My (re)presentation of the participants is mitigated by their own accounts, which they present in their own words.[5]

For the subaltern to have the possibility of speaking, it must be by changing the terms of language, speaking on one's own terms and for one's own purposes. Ultimately, Spivak looks for "slippage" in language, places of counternarrative as the spaces of resistance, where terms can be defined differently. Such counternarratives genuinely challenge dominant representations of the Other. Moments of slippage—or even stoppage—in language, when discourses are disputed and cannot be reconciled (this is Jean-François Lyotard's concept of *les différends*), are instances of turbulent flow, and it is within these moments that people might construct experience differently. This is where there may be possibility for the subaltern to speak.

Studying the writing of adult learners challenges all of us to read a different way because when the four participants restory, they are theorizing. The narratives are not a device to illustrate a theory residing outside of the text. Rather, I would ask that we listen for the analysis embedded within the narratives in much the same way that Krista Ratcliffe and Jacqueline Jones Royster insist that we must listen to our students: intently, honestly, and with the courage to continually interrogate our own assumptions as listeners and readers. One of the types of rhetorical listening that Ratcliffe identifies involves scholars and teachers seeking "opportunities for listening to the stories of others—all others" (39). Radical listening of this sort suggests a deeply reflective approach to the research process, which Royster and Gesa Kirsch term *strategic contemplation.* In defining her project of "listening to speak" to the subaltern woman, Spivak takes a similar position that she claims as the responsibility of female intellectuals. (See Chapters 2 and 3 for a fuller discussion of rhetorical listening and strategic contemplation.)

Conventional literacy narratives tout the goodness of literacy and its potential to convert struggling "illiterates" into more high-functioning contributors to society. Kirk Branch warns of the seductive power of the common literacy narrative, which simultaneously reifies a prevailing view of education as capable of creating an improved citizen and ignores the actual stories people have to report of pain or difficulties associated with their learning experiences ("In the Hallways," "What No Literacy Means"). The traditional literacy narrative, with its underlying goal of promoting mainstream literacy, may be important for maintaining support for social programs and agencies, but Branch warns of "romanticizing the experiences of these students beyond recognition" and in the process losing sight of the counternarratives people sometimes express ("In the Hallways" 16). What follows is an attempt to call attention to that restorying as a form of theorizing.

George calls it embarrassment, the particular exposure of a person caught naked without "word." Branch writes about the absence of literacy as a literacy event itself, highlighting the "control, domination, and/or oppression" that surrounds reading and writing, especially when they are denied ("What No Literacy Means" 53). Branch and I discuss this when we write a conversation together. He says: listen to adult learners because they are the real literacy theorists, exceeding the work of published scholars "in the form of the narrative, which come[s] laden with fairly detailed analysis and interpretation" (Rosenberg and Branch 125). The four participants' voices guide this book.

In the following chapters, then, I take up the task of "seeking to learn to speak (rather than listen to or speak for) the historically muted subject" in the way Spivak proposes, through an "unlearning" of privilege (295). This book features the participants speaking for themselves, often without my intrusion. Understanding their accounts relies on readers to interpret their words not simply as uncomplicated stories, or as the work of very basic writers, but as narratives that carry a significance that I do not wish to appropriate.

I think of the four participants in this book as intellectuals in the way that Gramsci believes ordinary people are capable of deep thought even when they are not attributed the social role of intellectual. He writes in *The Prison Notebooks* that "all men are intellectuals . . . but not all men have in society the function of intellectuals[;] . . . *homo faber* cannot be separated from *homo sapiens*." The one who works (the tool-bearer) is not disconnected from the one who knows (the thinker) (9). This idea of the people as intellectuals appears again in Spivak's push for the subaltern to represent herself and in Paulo Freire's argument ("Adult Literacy Process," *Pedagogy*) that education should be designed by the people based on what they know from their experiences as *thinkers*—a philosophy adopted by the Read/Write/Now center at its inception.[6]

I share the belief that ordinary people have the greatest knowledge of their own needs, and that they sometimes articulate that knowledge by theorizing about their literacy experiences. When I say that they are literacy theorists, I am obviously not referring to the kind of work that is done by professional intellectuals. I am not defining theory as abstract and generalizable. Theory is, in my view, about people challenging ideas, disrupting them, and finding a kernel of something else, that something that suggests a different way of looking at things based on a set of consistent guiding principles. When people articulate ideas that reflect those principles, and when they reach out to share their conceptual thinking about literacy with various publics, they act as theorists. The four participants theorize about literacy based on their experiences throughout the book and most explicitly in Chapter 5, where we see Violeta and Chief writing with the intent to persuade public audiences.

LAUREN: THIS LITERACY WORKER'S STORY

At first my students do service-learning projects with newly arrived immigrants in Bridgeport, Connecticut. Sometimes I go with them into the schools and community centers, where they mostly tutor or do child care. They bring the challenges of their experiences back to class, and this becomes the center of our discussions—the complexity of writing and assimilating: who gains literacy in a new country and who is denied. Along with my students, I volunteer, working with a Haitian woman who is learning to read and write in English. The woman I tutor has never been to school, has never written in her native Creole. She's older now, and as a nonliterate immigrant, the work she can get is cleaning tables and floors at Burger King. We meet at a Catholic agency that provides classes and child care to women and their children. Later we meet at the woman's home. Our sessions are difficult. She needs to pay bills and fill out medical forms. Both she and her husband have health problems. But gaining literacy is hard; the instructions on forms confuse her; she cannot remember how to spell *Bridgeport*. Even shaping letters on the page is a difficulty. We both feel frustrated when she cannot complete functional tasks. I begin to understand how it works: how nonliteracy, coupled with immigrant status (complicated by age, race, and poverty), maintains her habitus (Bourdieu, *Distinction*).

I meet another woman through a library ESL program. She is well employed as supervisor of a university food court, and she enjoys the benefits of middle-class life. Still, as a food service employee with basic literacy, she is locked in. She cannot advance to head chef, nor can she get out of kitchen work. Even though she has lived in the United States all her adult life and is a fluent speaker of English, her experience of quitting school in Korea in sixth grade leaves her feeling unable to learn. She has developed a system for seeking opportunities to gain literacy but then quitting as soon as she feels threatened. Our tutoring relationship goes on for four years. It is often turbulent because of her pattern of quitting and returning. During that time, I am a graduate student. I do a pilot study for a seminar on Kung Suk's cycle of pursuing and rejecting literacy instruction, and I learn that she is subjected to an ideology that excludes her as a semiliterate immigrant and also that she self-subjects, portraying herself as "stupid" in her own mind. She's acting out Foucault's two meanings of the word *subject:* "subject to someone else by control and dependence, and tied to his own identity by a conscience or self-knowledge. Both meanings suggest a form of power which subjugates and makes subject to" ("Subject" 212). By internalizing these contradictory definitions of discourse, Kung Suk simultaneously maintains and subjugates herself.[7] Her quitting cycle reflects Fanon's description of how colonialism is internalized as a force that one turns upon one's self. When confronting his Otherness in white culture, Fanon notices about the black man: "A feeling of inferiority? No, a feeling of nonexistence" (*Black Skin* 139). By the end of the project, I know that I will continue to work with adult learners, that I am compelled to understand the turbulent opposing impulses that draw people to literacy and also repel them.

I want to work with nonimmigrants, though, because gaining literacy in adulthood is a different problem when it is not about second language acquisition. Then it is about the politics of an educational system that has withheld its promise from some citizens. It is almost kept a secret that many Americans are unable to read and write. Victoria Purcell-Gates reflects on this when she writes about a mother and son who live in "a world without print." There is a good deal of reporting and analysis in adult basic education, but the topic of adult nonliteracy is rarely addressed in writing studies.

In this book, I deal with that absence and its effects—literacy when it is withheld—and what it means to gain literacy under unconventional circumstances. I write now to highly literate readers, people who make their living by words, by the power they possess to use, even play, with language. I want to tell you about the lives of people who come to writing and reading an alternate way because they value literacy differently from most of us. When I talk about my project with another community literacy researcher, someone who knows my work well, he gives me this imperative: No one has heard these people's voices. If you don't get them out there, they will continue to be unheard.

METHODS: USING NARRATIVE INQUIRY TO CONSTRUCT STORIES OF EVERYDAY LIVES

My fascination with the two immigrant tutees' relationships to literacy led me to a larger study of adult learners (all of them US citizens) who attend the Read/Write/Now Adult Learning Center. Learners go to this center by choice, unlike many programs where attendance is mandated by court order. Read/Write/Now is not a workplace training center, nor does it prepare students to take the GED exam. The curriculum is designed by individual teachers to reflect the interests that students express in their monthly written goal-setting statements. "People are serious here," the program coordinator, Pamela, told me when we first met. Despite the need of the center, like most programs, to satisfy some federal and state requirements for funding, she stressed that their overarching objective is to meet learners' individual wishes based on what learners deem relevant to their lives.

Going into a community in which I did not initially belong, I had the responsibility, like Shirley Brice Heath, Linda Flower, Ellen Cushman (*Struggle*), Caroline Heller, Paula Mathieu, and others who have done ethnographic literacy studies in communities beyond their own experience, of making the strange familiar (Sullivan). All of these women researchers have studied literacy practices in environments they approached as outsiders, whether their difference was marked by place, race, class, or gender (usually it was a combination). The eight months that I spent observing at Read/Write/Now before and during the data-collection period, plus the additional four years I spent volunteering at the center and conducting informal follow-up research, were important for establishing and maintaining relationships with the learners and teachers. I spent the first few months just getting a sense of the place, sitting in on classes and talking with people. Sometimes I took notes, but I was never anyone's teacher. As Cushman points out, the roles researchers inhabit in community settings can "contradict each other in important ways" ("Rhetorician" 21). How would it play out to be a hyperliterate researcher in a community of developing literates? A white woman from the university in a setting of working-class black, brown, and white people? Each time I walked through the doors of the library and entered the learning center, I was "the Other," yet in my academic work the people I studied became "other." Each time I changed roles, I was aware of my own shift in subject position. I am aware now of how the four participants take on a new role as the subjects of this book. Even though they represent themselves in their spoken and written narratives, I write along with them and am ultimately the author of this book. To what extent could my presentation of the people in this study benefit them, and to what extent was the knowledge I gained from them useful only to an academic community that kept them situated as Other?

I did not begin this research intending to study adults age forty and older; however, as I began to seek participants who had demonstrated that they would be reliable case studies, older learners emerged as the most stable population. Their teachers recommended them because of their dedication and reliability. Age turned out to be a significant factor in shaping the study since I was looking at a population for whom literacy was not conflated with work. Case studies of an older population allowed me to probe the question of motivation more deeply because participants were not constructing themselves primarily as workers.

This project went through two distinct phases. Most of the data were gathered during the initial period while I was visiting the center a couple of times a week. The four participants were involved in two interviews each, an initial discussion about their educational history and motivations for pursuing informal literacy instruction and a second discourse-based interview. The first interviews were all conducted at Read/Write/Now. The second interviews were designed for individual case studies based on their responses to the first interview and their writing samples. Most of these interviews were conducted at the participants' homes. I continued to collect writing samples from the participants throughout the time I knew them. For two people, George and Violeta, who volunteered to participate in a longitudinal study, this meant an additional two to four years. I also conducted interviews with their teachers.

Narrative inquiry was my primary methodology.[8] Rooted in narrative psychology, narrative inquiry operates from the premise that we craft our experiences by creating narratives to explain them and by listening to and living by the stories of others around us. As F. Michael Connelly and D. Jean Clandinin describe it, "a person is, at once, engaged in living, telling, retelling, and reliving stories" (4). According to narrative psychology, it is possible to therapeutically alter one's life by telling different, emotionally corrective narratives. Throughout my analysis, I used Connelly and Clandinin's concept of "restorying" to examine where participants were reacting to the turbulent flow of their own narratives and how they were respinning their experience by telling a different story.

The close reading of stories is a major analytical technique in psychology, philosophy, literature, anthropology, and other fields in which stories are examined repeatedly in varying contexts. Michel de Certeau explains that interpreting stories is the basis for theorizing about everyday life practices. Researchers rely on the case study and other ethnographic methods to provide narrative models on which to theorize; these narratives allow us to understand how people make knowledge in their everyday lives: "[In other words,] 'stories' provide the decorative container of a *narrativity* for everyday practices. . . . [T]hey represent a new variant in the continuous series of narrative documents. . . . A similar continuity suggests a certain *theoretical* relevance of narrativity so far as everyday practices are concerned" (70).

Working out experience by constructing narratives, and restor-
ing experiences through the act of restorying, is unique—often essential—to the act of writing. As it is remembered and retold, a
story changes, reshapes itself to meet shifts in the writer's sensibility,
an experience that is valued among experienced writers but brand
new for people who are just coming to writing. Victor Villanueva
reflects on the significance of reconstructing memory in narratives,
especially for people of color for whom individual identity is in-
fused with cultural memory. Noting that many other authors have
argued for "the need to reclaim a memory, memory of an identity in formation and constant reformation, the need to reclaim a
memory of an identity as formed through the generations," Villanueva indicates how writing can become a means of preserving
the memory of identity that has been shaped by colonization (12).
In Chapter 4, I examine the ways that the participants restory their
experiences, particularly as their representations of memory allow
them to create themselves as knowing subjects.

During the literacy history interviews, my objective was to find
out why the participants sought literacy as adults. I wanted to understand the purposes they believed writing served and how that
understanding had led them to Read/Write/Now. These interviews
provided a full literacy biography of each participant and a lens for
me to understand the themes in their written texts more fully. Everyone spoke extensively about a longtime desire to read and write
better. Their responses typically addressed material conditions in
their lives that had prevented them from becoming more literate
when they were young. Participants were especially enthusiastic
about telling the stories of their previous experiences with schooling. They were also willing to speak about their position as people
labeled "illiterate" and to discuss their reasons for wanting to read
and write better.[9] Besides questioning motives, some of my inquiry
pointed specifically to writing. In general, participants reported
that they did not use writing much outside of the program. Most
agreed that writing helped them to express themselves and also that
it could be a struggle.

The four participants' written texts and interview transcripts
were my main sources of data, and I analyzed the narratives from

the interviews and written texts against one another. I wanted to understand the connection between motivation and agency and how it is linked to power relations. To do this, I designed questions that probed areas of the first interviews where I thought participants might be articulating something more than a dominant narrative. Their texts especially suggested areas of possibility where they were expressing something in writing that was different from what they had said in interview responses. To thoroughly address the features of their writing, I shaped sections of the second interviews that pointed to individual pieces of writing in relation to other written texts and interview remarks.[10]

Connelly and Clandinin note that as research proceeds, participants and researchers engage in mutual storytelling. In their discoursal (second) interview, participants and I had a conversation about our previous conversation. My questions centered on participants' interpretation of their own texts and interview comments. Together we looked at pieces I had coded for various features that had emerged in the texts. Although the interpretation wasn't fully collaborative, I did include the participants in the process of analyzing their previous comments and writing (see Chapter 3, in which I talk with participants about their interview transcripts, especially the section on George's discoursal interview). In this way, I was able to dig deeper into their purposes and speak with them about impulses underlying the ambitions they expressed.

In his book on in-depth interviewing, Irving Seidman considers the ethical dilemmas and implications of the interview process and especially the relationship that develops between interviewer and participant. Although interviewers typically gain more than their participants in terms of the products of the interview, Seidman explains that there is something significant for the participant that is often overlooked. This is "the type of listening the interviewer brings to the interview. It takes the participants seriously, values what they say, and honors the details of their lives" (92). By attempting to listen without interruption or to steer the conversation, I hoped to acknowledge that each person's experience had worth. The program coordinator and the teachers at Read/Write/Now also encouraged this process. When they recommended case study participants, they spoke about the benefits their students would gain. It was apparent to them that the opportunity for adult learners to participate in interviews and to have conversations about their writing would be validating.

Once I had finished observing and interviewing, my role at the center shifted from researcher-observer to volunteer. By that time, I was a familiar face, and I came in periodically to help with writing projects. I would speak with people about their writing and review drafts with them; however, I kept some distance so that none of the learners at Read/Write/Now would think of me as their teacher or tutor. I didn't want to reproduce the traditional power dynamic of the educated outsider who has knowledge to impart to the poor "illiterates." By maintaining instead a casual relationship with learners, I was able to interact with them primarily as a researcher who was interested in listening to their stories rather than as a bearer of academic knowledge.

For more than four years after the original data collection, I continued a longitudinal case study with George. A couple of years into this project, another of the participants, Violeta, returned to Read/Write/Now after "stopping out"[11] for a time, and she rejoined my study. This second phase involved one or two interviews a year and ongoing collection of George and Violeta's new writing. During this extended period, I incorporated grounded theory (Charmaz) as an additional methodology because it provided a lens for approaching the data again. As I added new texts and transcripts, I picked up threads of the research that I had not yet analyzed, and I looked for shifts in participants' writing and sense of themselves. The longitudinal studies ended when George and Violeta stopped attending Read/Write/Now for reasons unrelated to my project. In all, I worked directly with learners for more than five years, nearly a year for the original study and about four years for the longitudinal project.

What started out as four case studies changed. Initially, I collected the participants' narratives as data, I coded for themes that emerged in their writing, and I reshaped my interpretation based on what they had to say. But the material took on other meanings as I used it for presentations and articles. In each new form, with every rhetorical purpose, the analysis changed. The value of the four people's texts changed. I changed. I continued visiting the center and talking with learners about their writing. What started out as a research study ended up as an engaged conversation with these four participants. Even now, when I revisit their transcripts and our discussions of their writing, I can ask myself: What's there that I haven't noticed before? How do I restory the participants' accounts as I continue to shape the narrative of my relationship to them and my own story as researcher, theorist, and teacher? I am not apart *from* but a part *of* the stories. This book is my story of their stories.

COMMUNITY LITERACY PERSPECTIVES

Within writing studies, community literacy researchers make the distinctive argument that we pay careful attention to the words of people outside of the formal institutions that ignore their experiences and constrain their voices (George; Gere; Goldblatt, *Because*; Grabill; Parks; Rousculp). Linda Flower distinguishes community literacy from other "discourses of engagement" because of its commitment to exploring discourse "with" and "for" others, rather than representing people by folding their views into existing discourses (2, 19). I agree with Flower's imperative, that community members must convey their concerns in their own voices. The four people I focus on have taught me more from their narratives about how nonliteracy operates and why they now take action to resist their positioning than I could know from another source. Through the process of challenging the scripts imposed on them by restorying their narratives, they theorize about their own experiences, thus moving toward the "rhetorical agency" that Flower claims is attainable.

Other community literacy researchers such as Paula Mathieu also stress the need for critical, honest engagement with those whose experiences are outside of the mainstream and whose voices are usually unheard. In the Chicago-based StreetWise writers group that she researched, vendors who sold street newspapers, many of whom were homeless themselves or who had been homeless, met to discuss the social and political issues they wanted to make public in their writing. Mathieu shows how by representing their own concerns in their own writing, vendors provided themselves the "hope" of making changes within their own communities. Concern for the knowledge that people create when they represent themselves is common among community literacy researchers, though competing pressures to comply with their sponsoring agents make it difficult for literacy programs to keep their attention focused solely on learners' wishes. Jeffrey Grabill makes the important point that literacy programs, whether institutionally or community sponsored, usually "enforce this separation between literacy and life by the ways in which we design literacy programs because we rarely ask students and workers what they need. We rarely ask them to make their lived experiences the center of our collective educational experience" (x).

I engaged with learners in a community outside of formal schooling because I wanted to understand how "literacy and life" are linked. Through their writing and their oral critique, the participants who tell their stories in this book create narratives of resistance in which they become able to revise their own lives and influence the ways they are gazed upon by others. They do this by telling what Flower calls the "story-behind-the-story" through the act of restorying, which does more than expose: it recasts the terms of experience and in this way has the potential to disrupt dominant literacy narratives and create the possibility for social change.

LIVING A LIFE OF VALUE

Adult learners are already critical subjects. Their understanding of how they are affected by power may be enhanced by their education, and their literacy studies will certainly give them tools for articulating their knowledge differently (Cushman, *Struggle*), but they are not unknowing dupes who need to be taught how to evaluate their experiences, as some critical theorists suggest. Their critical awareness confirms Freire's assertion that the oppressed understand the motivations of the oppressor; adult literacy learners already possess "their own thought-language at the level of their perception of the world" ("Adult Literacy Process" 619).

One example that has particularly encouraged my research is Caroline Heller's study of the Tenderloin Women Writers' Workshop in San Francisco. The workshop writers wanted to change conditions for people in their neighborhood, and a few of them consciously sought to influence local public policy. But Heller observed that for the most part, the women writers "came to the workshop not to change the world or even to complain about it. They came to be reassured that they had lived lives that were of value and that could be—through the precision of their own words—felt, understood, and remembered by others" (18). In Heller's writing group, and in their classes at Read/Write/Now, people engage in a community where they are reassured and affirmed. For adult learners, a profound aspect of their education is the validation they gain when they begin to identify as literate. Their work with the student-centered curriculum at Read/Write/Now, their interactions with peers and teachers, and their writing and discussions all contribute to a revised sense of self in which they come to acknowledge that they are not "dummies." Instead, they interact in an environment in which their intelligence is recognized rather than denigrated.

Mathieu and Heller both call attention to the "conflicts of identity" that many people grapple with as writers. The competing impulses they struggle with in their lives are not distinguishable from the conflicts they bring to their literacy studies. This again is the turbulent flow of material and ideological conditions that bubbles up in the form of conflicting discourses when they write. It is what makes their desire for literacy so complicated and so important.

I have found, as others have (see Cuban; Daniell; Horsman; Ray; Rockhill; Sohn), that the yearning for reassurance that they have "lived lives that were of value" is especially meaningful for adults who are in a reflective phase of their lives. The four participants you will meet in this book already have a perspective from which they examine culture, and especially their own subject position as nonliterates. What they are lacking are the rhetorical tools to speak out and publicly acknowledge their position. The narratives that Violeta, Lee Ann, George, and Chief share about their experiences with education, work, parenting, and society exceed the boundaries of what critical literacy can tell us. They also exceed the work of other community studies that have theorized about learners' lives more than they have considered the participants themselves as experts who can theorize about their own literacy. By acknowledging the ways they construct their everyday experiences, we can get to know adult learners better as authors whose wisdom informs their determination to gain and use their literacy.

Violeta, Lee Ann, George, and Chief: they unfold their stories throughout the following chapters. By listening to these participants speak, we can move beyond conventional expectations of the meanings and purposes of literacy and rely on their words as our models when we shape our literacy programs and curricula.

2

Speaking from "the Silent, Silenced Center": "Just Because You Can't Read Doesn't Mean That You Don't Know"

BY READING ADULT LEARNERS' WORDS ON their terms, we can learn to understand literacy differently. This involves the close listening and sustained attention that Royster, Ratcliffe, and other feminist scholars have termed *rhetorical listening*. Ratcliffe explains that the act of rhetorical listening "turns *intent* back on the listener, focusing on listening *with intent* to hear troubled identification, instead of listening *for intent* of an author" (46, emphasis in original). Intention on the part of the listener is what Spivak claims we need if the subaltern is to find a voice beyond her immediate community. Readers must take seriously the "the silent, silenced center" representing their own experience. As Royster insists in "When the First Voice You Hear Is Not Your Own," there remains a need for more honest critical "action in cross-boundary exchange" (30). Our goal as researchers can—should—be to give that attention to people's accounts of their experiences, as well as in our gathering and interpreting of data and in reporting it. Later in this chapter, for example, I present an incident when Lee Ann told me to put her story in the newspaper. She practically insisted that my job was to circulate her story to the public. That was the role she was putting me in as the witness to her experiences.

I open this chapter with Royster and Ratcliffe's arguments in mind. In the narratives you are about to read, I am the audience, the listener, even as I introduce the participants and explain the context of their narratives. This chapter is about the experience of nonliteracy as told from the perspectives of the four participants—

the self-representations of those at the "silent, silenced center." The way they are represented here is the representation they have chosen to offer about their backgrounds, their lives, and their work. Ratcliffe proposes that we listen differently to understand the interchange between self and other as a way to better listen and respond to the discourses people articulate when they speak on their own terms (26). She flips the word "*understanding*" so that we have to interrogate it more closely as "standing under" the discourses of another: "Standing under discourses means letting discourses wash over, through and around us and then letting them lie there to inform our politics and ethics" (28). In other words, as rhetorical listeners we should not be quick to interpret and decide; instead, we can remain with others, experiencing their discourses as they choose to present them.

∽

In (re)presenting the four participants' narratives, I want to "stand under" their discourses and let them wash over me. And I want those discourses—their words—to wash over readers too. Because, as Ratcliffe explains, "Standing under the discourses of others means first, acknowledging the existence of these discourses; second, listening for (un)conscious presences, absences, unknowns; and third, consciously integrating this information into our world views and decision making" (29). These terms—"standing under" and "washing over"—suggest a model of how to do rhetorical listening. And so, in my effort to listen without appropriation, to allow my thinking to be transformed by the words of others presenting themselves, I keep the processes these terms offer as the actions of listening at the front of my mind. I invite readers to step back and bear witness without judgment, to listen by doing nothing. In this way, you and I can try to understand nonliteracy in the way of people who have lived that experience.

Because I "stand under" the four participants, I use italics to indicate my voice throughout Chapters 2 and 3. In this way, I become the Other. My voice is marked as different. The four participants are the Self, the dominant speakers, who are represented by the standard font. I do not quote from them in these chapters¹—they are not subordinate to the author—rather, theirs are the primary voices, and I am secondary.

VIOLETA

I keep it pinned to the bulletin board over my desk: a flier with Violeta's picture on it that reads "20 Years of Learning and Growing at Read/ Write/Now!" Hers is the image advertising the literacy center. She is pretty, with black hair and delicate features, a calm but intent expression on her face. She wears a filmy white sweater. Violeta is looking down at a book open on the table; her hands are settled on the book, but they are not resting. They are bent at the wrists, the fingers pressing into the pages, guiding her. Her vision falls onto the open book, her place kept by the frame of her fingers. There is a wrinkle between Violeta's brows, an arrow pointing to her pressed lips.

But once I get to know Violeta, I start to see her face differently. The photo does not reveal the expression in her eyes or the tired pouches that surround them. Even though she appears to be a young woman on the flier, her eyes, if they were looking at the camera, would reveal a woman older than her forty years. Her cheeks draw in to meet the cast of her eyes, the serious gaze, the intent reader. This is Violeta reading, caught up in a moment when she can turn inward and care for herself.

She is from Puerto Rico and has lived most of her life on the Island. But there has always been some back and forth. When they were in New York, her mother would sometimes enroll her in school. Violeta enjoyed school. The family was always moving, though, and most of the time as the eldest child she was made to stay home to care for younger siblings. In Puerto Rico, her stepfather, a trash collector and a drug addict, kept her literally locked inside the house, preventing Violeta from going out in the world and getting an education. She speaks of learning to read and write as "a door open" or "no door closed." She means this literally as well as metaphorically.

Like everyone I meet at Read/Write/Now, Violeta describes acquisition of literacy as access to school:

My mother never liked to put me in school in Puerto Rico. I don't know why. When I was sixteen, and then I decide to go. But it was little bit, not too much. I be in school more in New York, in

Manhattan. My mother, we live over there when we get over there. My mother was putting me only in an English, like third grade. And then she has to go back to Puerto Rico, taking me out in the—. And then when we get to Puerto Rico, I never have school. That's confuse me. A lot.

All the back and forth between Puerto Rico and New York and between Spanish and English made, and continues to make, it difficult for Violeta to know which language to use.

I do it much better reading and writing in English. Not very well in Spanish. But in math, I do it much better in Spanish than English. . . . It's hard when I go into the classroom, the math. I know what's the number exactly, but I don't know how to say it in English. I know how to say it in Spanish. Writing and reading, I do more in English. But my writing is okay, reading is okay. Nothing in Spanish. I go into church, right? And I have to first, you know, read the Bible. I praying to God to not to teach [to teach] me how to read the Bible. I don't know how to read the Bible in Spanish. It is very hard for me, but in English it is more easy for me. And I get through.

Confusion over schooling: When can you have it? When can you not? School was inconsistently available. Everyone I talked with recalled school as a place she or he had access to only sometimes. Violeta remembers being confused; Lee Ann remembers feeling unable to concentrate; Chief will think of school as a wonderful place where he wished he could spend his days, while George will associate schooling with hunger and terrible weather. No matter the conditions of their individual lives, school was always out of reach. And even if you could go one day, the opportunity to learn might be taken away the next.

Since Violeta lives far from most of her relatives, maintaining her relationships with them matters a lot. Writing and reading letters on her own is one of her main reasons for pursuing literacy. When other people read your mail for you, they know the intimate news of your life before you do. Not knowing how to read, she explains,

It's very sad for me. And then I ask to the neighbor to read my letter when it was convenient, you know what I mean? The other people know before they know me before go in that letter, you know? That's making me turn to over here to learn. I want to read my own letter and everything.

Violeta says she wants to read her letters. She wants to write in her portfolio, which she refers to as her "life book." She wants to show her children that she can "depend about myself" *and does not need the help of others. I hear her express so much desire that is motivating her to learn and to study, and that yearning grows as she continues to pursue what she wants for herself.*

I want to learn more, like I say before. I can help my kid with the homework, paper reading, and I do a mom and dad [*meaning she is a single mother*], and I running the house and everything. And I has to learn, you know, read paper, like my bill was on time, before I don't know how to read my appointment, the bill. Or the teacher would send a letter for me about the children home school now. I learning about how to read it, how to depend about myself. . . . I know how to read the letter now. 'Bout my appointment, how I couldn't read my appointment. When I going to do some appointment, they giving me some paper to sign, I want to learn what kind of paper did I put my sign? To read exactly. That's why one of the reason that I do this. Yup.

Violeta pours us large glasses of pineapple juice with lots of ice. It is going to be another hot day. The doors and windows are open, but because it is morning, the street noise is so quiet you might not know you are in an apartment in the projects. Soon her youngest son appears on his tricycle, riding through the apartment and demanding his mami's attention. Violeta gets frustrated with him and the trike in the house and calls upstairs to an older son, who comes down to mind his brother by flipping on the TV. Violeta and I stay in the kitchen, where we talk despite the interruptions of all ages of children, all of who want something from Mami.

Violeta has six children and two grandchildren. When she and her children moved to Springfield, her social worker helped Violeta to realize that as a primary caregiver she was entitled to an education while receiving public assistance. Violeta connects her decision to attend Read/ Write/Now to the loss of a baby at that time: "I no having school for long time, and then when my baby passed away, I decide to come back to school; that's when I know the program." *For her, approaching literacy was connected to her decision to raise her children on the US mainland rather than in Puerto Rico. The combined support of her social worker and an "Americano" boyfriend made it possible for her to take care of her family while also attending the program where she could get the education she had always wanted.*

But caring for herself as a student is not always easy. Her life gets in the way. Violeta's little son left the Head Start program he was enrolled in, and that meant that Violeta had to leave Read/Write/Now too. She was gone for a couple of years, sometimes in contact with the center, always with the intention of returning. One day when I came in to assist with a writing project, Violeta was back, and she asked me right away whether we could do research together again.

During the six years that I knew her, Violeta "stopped out" and "stopped back in" a couple of times based on her children's needs. She also took time off to visit her family in Puerto Rico and to pursue a romantic relationship there. Each time she returns to the center she is embraced as a beloved member of the community and a serious learner who has returned to continue her studies. I opened this section with a description of her image on the Read/Write/Now flier to illustrate Violeta's tenacious approach to literacy. When we talk, she always mentions her progress as a learner and how she must juggle studying with taking care of her children. I get to know her determination as an intrinsic part of her. Later, in Chapter 5, she describes Rosa Parks, a woman she admires for never giving up. That is how I would describe Violeta. The impulse to care for herself in a setting that is apart from her home and child care responsibilities is one of the primary motivations that keeps her coming back to the center. Violeta views literacy as the one gift she can give herself separate from caring for others, and she sees this form of self-care as essential to being a mother, a woman, and a member of society.

CHIEF

When I ask him about a name to use in my research, he tells me, "I do have a nickname that my friends call me: Chief. You can call me Chief." *It is inscribed on the flower boxes that hang beneath the front windows of his home: "Chief," in neat light blue script on white wooden boxes. His house sits on a manicured plot in a shade-filled neighborhood on the east edge of town closest to the suburbs. It is a cozy place, where he lives with his wife. Their children are grown, but they all live nearby. Chief has been watching the news on TV while he waits for me to arrive for our interview. He turns it off and gives me a tour that features stories of the people in framed photos in the living room: children, grandchildren, and many friends, including the men in his gospel singing groups. He shows me his vegetable garden out back, and we chat about growing greens and tomatoes in New England.* "I'm going to cut my grass after a while," *he says, gazing skyward, considering the thunderstorm predicted for later that evening, and then looking down at the well-tended plants in his grassy backyard.*

Raised on a sharecropper's farm in rural, pre–Civil Rights South Carolina, Chief began working alongside his father and other family members at a young age. His brother was married when Chief was about ten, and so, as the second oldest son, Chief took on the responsibilities of "plowing and mule[ing], and helping my father . . . cutting wood for the fire," *which prevented him from attending school regularly. They had two fields, a large field a distance from the house where the men and boys worked and a closer field where the women and girls farmed in addition to maintaining the home. When Chief did go to school, it was usually on rainy days or in winter. Then he walked two to three miles each way. It was a long walk, and fights broke out along the road:*

We had to fight 'cause the blacks and whites would both go [to the same school]. We'd have to fight for the little ones and the girls. Then they got buses, but we're still walking.

Everyone had to work. The boys had to go out with their father every morning. Yet some bodies—female bodies—were less necessary for farm work and more available to become schooled. But even the girls were able to get only some *more schooling than the boys, and they had to be crafty about it. Chief and his brothers would cover their sisters' chores so that the girls could attend school. When his daddy wasn't looking, Chief and his brothers and his mother would help to sneak one sister past their father's gaze and off to school:*

We sort of looked out for her. Because we was wanting them to get—ah, at least get a—go to school. But when she came from school, she would really work hard making sure, my daddy, a lot of time, didn't know she was going to school. He [Daddy] thought he was—you see, my father was like this. He said, "One kid has to stay out." He figured that, uh, the other one has to stay out to do the work around the house because when we go out—we had a farm like, a field, a farm that's well over, maybe two miles from the house. Then my sisters and my mother and them would work on the cotton around the house, at the house, while the menfolk would go two miles to the other field.

And, uh, so, my mother and sisters would stay here, would see when the bus was coming (when we did get it), the bus was coming that-a-way. The bus was coming; my sister would be in the ditch; come and hide. She had to hide behind a bush. She was scared my father would look back and see her coming up to catch the bus.

We would tell her: "One be sitting on the seat." We'd tell her to do that when Daddy got ready to turn.

Some[times] he'd say, "What you making motions at?"

"I'm playing with my brothers on the back of the wagon!"

We'd always been like real close-knit family and we look out for one another, so we wanted our sisters to get, go to school even if we couldn't. And she, my mother, would help her to get, do the work. So they would, they did it sure en[ough].

Then, on Sundays, the sisters would help their brothers read in church:

I would sit with my sisters, somebody that knew how to read. My sisters and them could read because they went to school more than we did, so we would work with them and they would work with us.

The girls went to school, and later, some of the girls went to college. They're still close, Chief and all his siblings. And even though Chief couldn't go to school, his children did. One of his daughters was studying to be a minister and another is married to a minister. The ones who didn't get consistent schooling, or who had less of an opportunity for an education, Chief took care of himself. He brought his grandson with him to a family literacy program at Read/Write/Now. He brought one brother with him to the center for a while. Maybe he pushed them too strongly, he recalls. His regret about his own inability to get an education is so intense that he insists that others value and pursue literacy. I hear it when he talks to younger learners in a harsh tone; his words are threaded with his own resentment toward people who have the chance to learn but aren't taking their studies seriously enough. I see it in the swell of his cheeks and the way he looks down when he speaks to them, his anger and regret bubbling below the surface. He may say a few hard words, but most of the emotion he keeps in.

He has always known how to work hard. For many years, Chief was a welder and a forklift operator. He had a career and provided for his family. The house he bought in Springfield was not the first he owned. He purchased his first home in South Carolina, a large brick house, when he was seventeen. In certain ways, Chief has led a mainstream life. He takes vacations with his wife. He is involved in his church and other communities. After he was disabled in a motorcycle accident that injured his back, and he could no longer do the work he used to do, Chief could devote himself to being a student.

I always wanted to read and write. I didn't get the chance. . . . You always wanted to learn to read. Especially, if when you don't grow up and you—, it helps you to better yourself in jobs, to speak better, and it helps you in a lot of ways. I love to read now; since I learned to read, I read all the time. And it's opened up a new world for me.

Even when they didn't have school, Chief and his brothers and cousins did have other kinds of learning, and knowledge wasn't limited to work. I ask him how he thinks literate people see those who don't know how to read and write.

A lot of people look down on 'em, but they shouldn't look down; they don't even know the people's backgrounds. . . . But you know what? What I even have had people say? "You don't know how to read; you're stupid." That don't make you stupid because you don't know how to read. You got, uh, we call it "mother wits." [It] is more smarter than the man that got all the education in the world. Because we used to, uh, me and my oldest brother . . . we used to go out at night and spend the whole night out in the woods, hunting. And, uh, it don't take education to do that. You gotta have sense. [There are] wild snakes, and, down there they got a lot of poison snakes, that live in the swamp. You could live off the fat of the land. We used to . . . we could live with that and then have to go without seeing a city for days and nights, or whatever. Gotta learn how to hunt. Learn how to live. Make traps to catch wild game. We have done that, lived that kind of life. . . . I be just like a wild man. I don't know, I probably couldn't survive [now], but back then I could. You have to know what kind of berries to eat in the woods. Ah, you even eat plants.

On the day when I went to his house for an interview, Chief recalled what being nonliterate was like:

It's a, uh, a shyness from when you, ah, can't read and write. . . . You set back and let a lot of other people do the talking because you don't say too much. . . . Uh, you don't want to say the wrong thing. Ah, you get some of the words, big words that are said you don't understand. So you don't want to say nothing that you don't know what you're talking about. . . . Opinions. . . They might not, uh, even if they don't know you can't read, you still be thinking: my opinion don't mean nothing here.

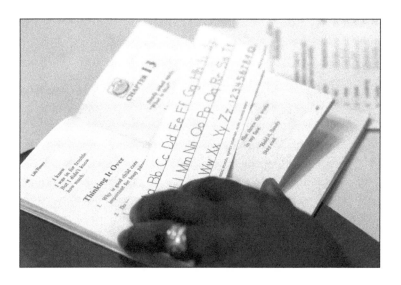

Underneath the joy he expresses over reading and writing, Chief describes his frustration too. I take in his sense of conflict and regret when his voice becomes low and he looks down. He gets upset when he recalls the past and the losses he experienced, some because of nonliteracy and some because of the conditions of his life. When he articulates regret, his words rumble. I hear the "set[ting] back" he talks about as reticence mixed with sadness. But these words come from a man whose opinions do matter, who knows now (at least much of the time and after many years of uncertainty) that people do want to hear what he has to say. Now people will listen to him and acknowledge that he knows. Yet for most of his life, Chief has wrestled with his "shyness" and turned it in upon himself. Even when he knew what he thought and wanted to express, he still self-censored because of his anxiety about saying "the wrong thing" and appearing ignorant. The stigma he bore as someone who knew some of the words but might not understand the big words caused him repeatedly to doubt his own ability to contribute in conversations. Because he feared that others might judge his opinions as irrelevant, Chief was caught in a cycle of self-doubting and imagining that he was doubted, which rendered him essentially silent.

LEE ANN

Outspoken and abrupt, Lee Ann is the person I hear first when I enter the literacy center. Her raspy voice precedes her. It fills the air that separates the "developing" readers and writers classroom from the general space of the center. Lee Ann offers her spoken narratives to whoever will listen. She is talking about Jesus, about money, about how she got here this morning, what she ate for dinner, and then back to the Lord. When I see Lee Ann, she is digging through her purse and pulling out a stack of bills. She holds onto them with both hands. She has brought her bills with her to Read/Write/Now because she wants help sorting them. She wants to separate the bills from the junk.

Lee Ann recalls her school experiences:

We were poor, moved to place to place, okay? Lucky we had a place to sleep, never mind to go to school. So by me getting shifted around, it, it was hard to get, go to school. Half the time I didn't go because I was dirt poor. So we had to move around from place to place; when we didn't pay the rent, we got kicked out. So me, my sister, and I and [unclear], ain't none of my family learned to really read, you know. Lucky we survived, you know. And, uh, then when I was sixteen years old or, uh, uh, I went to the, uh, Chester Street School. They put you in a special class, where there was no special learning back in my day. I'm sixty years old. Back there, there was nothing that they got today to help a person like me. So, what happened was, uh. So, when I was sixteen, I wasn't getting anywhere. You know, I wasn't getting nowhere. I wasn't learning nothing. It was stupid for me to go. I quit at sixteen. This is it. You know, you know. I am wasting their time. They're wasting my time. There was no—, and I wasn't, you know. So I just gave up and quit and went and got a job.

Work was Lee Ann's only choice when school failed her. For most of her adult life, Lee Ann did janitorial work, either as a housekeeper in people's homes or in office buildings. No matter the setting, bosses denigrated her. She was at her last job cleaning a public building for nine years. Ten would have gotten her pension benefits from the city. I asked Lee Ann whether any employers had an interest in her becoming more literate:

Ugh! I was a housekeeper. They didn't give a darn. I was a housekeeper. As long as you could clean a toilet and mop a floor, what did they give you? Right, huh!

Lee Ann experiences painful oppositions. The contradictory behaviors of individuals and institutions surround her. She gets "kicked to the curb" but refuses to stay there. "I'm going to still be a fighter here," she insists. When Lee Ann talks about work, she describes it as both a mark of independence (she makes her own financial decisions, such as whether to go back to work now or to retire) and of oppression (her nonliteracy locks her into menial, physically draining labor). She wrestles with these contradictory aspects of her life as a nonliterate individual.

Work, the alternative to schooling: default, subsistence, validation. Lee Ann has worked from age sixteen to sixty without a break. She has raised her children, bought and sold houses. She maintains three properties and negotiates with her relatives, who inhabit them. She will tell you who is and is not paying their bills. Lee Ann talks about possible transactions she might make as she waves around the collection of bills she carries in her large bag. Financial headaches, home ownership, the responsibility of difficult relatives. Children and now grandchildren. How can she purchase real estate when she is unable to do the paperwork? I don't know how she did it, or if she really did it, or what she actually did and did not do. But I am pretty sure that I believe her, because Lee Ann is not afraid to ask friends and relatives for help. She will ask a stranger too if she wants something bad enough.

Lee Ann is a white woman of sixty, wide, with shoulders that rise up around her neck. Although she rarely stops talking and often places herself uncomfortably close to others, she also comes and goes with purposeful movement. I become accustomed to Lee Ann's blend of raw truth and evangelical rhetoric, her rambling, the fever pitch of her voice. She says, "All my life I've got to do hard labor. Walmart was going to hire me, but I can't read the coupons." *She makes this and other remarks forcefully, as though she wants them to pierce the listener, and I am drawn in by her candor.*

Still, she says, learning is a challenge. Even after leaving school at sixteen, Lee Ann would periodically enroll in one of the adult learning programs in Springfield. Although she claims that none of her adult basic education experiences was particularly inadequate, she did not seem to be "getting it." *Until enrolling at Read/Write/Now, she was stuck with a view of herself as unable to retain what she learned. It's different at this center, she says; the teacher, Carolyn, is good.*

It wasn't just her feelings of disability that victimized Lee Ann. She remembers growing up "negative" *in poverty in a troubled family with an alcoholic father and an incompetent mother:*

My mother told me, and you know, told me I was retarded at times.

Lee Ann's mother refused to give her reading materials or anything linked to learning:

When I was going to the store with my mother, begging her for a book, and she: "You don't need that." My mother, a book or something like that, a little kiddie book like you buy your kids? And she said, "Yeah, you don't need that."

But you wanted it?

Oh, yeah! With all my heart's desire I wanted it. You know? Like I say, she didn't care if I got a education, you know? Didn't want me to have a little book to read.

Sorting out Lee Ann's stories is complicated. Who can know why her mother denied her books? Lee Ann suggests that her mother was unable to care adequately for herself or her children. I remember her telling me that her mother, an extremely large woman, didn't own a bra. When Lee Ann tells me this detail, it hits home: the family was destitute. Literacy was just another thing they could not have. But I can tell by the way Lee Ann spits out her mother's remark, "Yeah, you don't need that," that she understands it as a judgment of Lee Ann. Either her mother truly believed that Lee Ann was incapable of learning, or she had invented the notion that her child, like herself, must remain non-literate. In Lee Ann's memory, as I hear it retold in our conversations, poverty and nonliteracy are conflated: the family was poor, so no one could read. Her sister, the only literate member of the family, taught herself to read later in life. One of the ways Lee Ann reacted to her mother's denial of reading materials was to become a hoarder of books.

Literacy appears in unconventional forms in Lee Ann's experience. She piles books in her garage and in plastic bags in the closet. But it's not only books and reading that matter to her. She also talks about driving in a way that overlaps with reading and writing. One day during class, when the group has digressed into a conversation about learning to drive, Lee Ann blurts, "We all don't read good, but we're sitting here with driver's licenses. You want something bad, you go out and get it." *A few years earlier, Lee Ann had gotten her license,[2] which she considered one of the great achievements of her life. Once she had obtained it, she had a new sense of her own independence. Ironically (and perhaps not merely coincidentally), driving took Lee Ann to Read/Write/Now. She recounts how she first came to the library-based center about a year earlier:*

Well, I came—you know how I got to actually come here? I was giving—I help people out a lot. I was giving the neighbor a ride to bring her books back. She lives down my street. And I said, "You know, I wonder if they got anything?" 'Cause a lot of the time they have something for the library. So I turn around, and I went into the, into the, and I went to bring my friend back that lives in the trailer park. I said, "Yeah, right around the corner." The lady in the library said, "Right over here." So then I, then I come in here and investigate. And I talked to Melissa [*a teacher*]. And she pulled out the paper and then turned around and said: Well, when they get a spot for me, they'll call me.

Whether or not Lee Ann already knew that her local library offered a program for adult learners is irrelevant. Perhaps she knew and her trip to the library was more deliberate than she lets on. What matters is that she did it. She entered the library and inquired about its services. Walking inside a library for the first time was a major step for her, as it is for many of the learners at the center—to enter the building, the home of books, this foreign land that would become the place where she would soon go three days a week, every week, month after month, because now was the time to study. This was the first time in Lee Ann's life that she could sustain herself as a student. Learning, for Lee Ann, is a break from work.

Now I am retired. I ain't tuckered out from slaving working for somebody else. I can come here, and 9:30 is good for me, for the hours, you know? And like I said, and then go home and I am rested, and I'm—. I don't have to kill myself coming here. And, you know, I have more time to study and stuff. When you're tired out by working, how can you study, right?

It is a blazing August morning. I follow Lee Ann's good directions to the urban trailer park where she lives, just a mile away from Read/Write/ Now and off the same service road, turn in before the Pep Boys, and enter the neighborhood behind the commercial strip, the constructed blocks of rectangular metal and vinyl buildings set onto small plots. Lee Ann is out front to greet me, and she enthusiastically gives me a tour. We start on the enclosed porch, which she has transformed into a storage area. It is filled with trash bags. These contain things that Lee Ann claims she needs to sort through and give away. She points to boxes of mail, everything from supermarket circulars to newspapers to bills stacked together. Because she cannot distinguish between junk and important correspondence, Lee Ann saves everything. The house itself, though dense with photographs, tchotchkes, and shelves packed with books, is tidy. It is clean. I understand now that she spends a good deal of time gathering and sorting, endlessly attempting to work through mounds of stuff and text to find clarity. Lee Ann leads me back outside and across the street where the trash is set out for pickup. She wants to show me the books she has thrown away. She wants me to see that there is resolution in this process, that she makes decisions about what can go. She opens her trash can and starts pulling out the discarded stuff because there may be something I want. She unearths a volume from an old Time Life series. This one is on anatomy. Lee Ann opens it to a page of diagrams of the penis, suggesting I might be interested in this. I might find it useful.

Back inside we sit in her kitchen with the air conditioner on. Lee Ann plugs in a decorative tabletop fountain that lights up and circulates a stream of water. She talks about her collections of books:

I got books; I used to, to go to tag sales and all the time my kids would say—and I got a whole big wall of books and books and books, right? They would say, "You going to a tag—bringing more home, more books, you can't read what you got, all them more books!" You know, bringing all those books home? [*She laughs.*] And I said, "Well, you know, maybe." I had a wishful: maybe someday. And this is the closest, this year I got. And I think maybe this is my year here at Reading/Write/Now. Yeah.

Lee Ann imagines books have a certain power because of the wisdom that might be locked between their covers, offering secrets to understanding the world. She picks up a Ziploc bag of religious booklets that she has brought into the kitchen to show me:

Oh, these are my pride! I got these brand new! . . . These are my jewels, I'll tell you! Keep the devil at bay.

The booklets, which she purchased in the 1970s while on a religious crusade, have taken on value for Lee Ann because of the wisdom she believes they contain.

See this one here? Yeah. Oh, you got to see this one. You got to see this one. This is the, the best one. That the church sent me. This is the best! This is the best! This is the best! I didn't know how valuable this was 'til somebody read this one day for me. Yeah, I had it amongst my stuff, didn't know how valuable this was 'til somebody read a little bit of it, try to take this book, and I say: "Oh, you're not getting my book! Not getting this one." Now I know how valuable this is! This is all about the pyramids!

When I sit with Lee Ann in her kitchen, talking with her as she continues to bring out more and more books to display, I finally understand that collecting books allows her to fill a material and emotional ✓ *hole. Her comments about the books and about a neighbor who used to read to her "'cause she was, like, able"* allow me to see that Lee Ann's *desire is to take in the knowledge on the page. She imagines that accumulating books will help her to amass knowledge. She also wants the independence that literacy promises. Independence for Lee Ann began with driving, which gave her the ability to take control of her life and help out other people rather than being dependent on them. In the same way, reading provides an avenue for participating in society differently,* ✓ *as someone who can assist others and not be a drain on them.*

GEORGE

In the opening of Chapter 1, George reflected on the power of literacy. Now he tells his own story:

You see, well, everybody that lived down in South Carolina, some people was fortunate enough that, uh, they had their own farm, and their kids could go to school. And some people didn't. And I was one of the unfortunate one that, you know, me and my family we was, lived on someone else place, you know, at the time. And, um, you know, living on someone else place, working for them, you know, you pay your rent out of that. You know what I mean? So, you most likely—I'm being honest with you—as far as I can remember it's almost like with slavery time because you most have to do what, you know, the person that place that you living on, what they want you to do. That's one of the reasons why I couldn't go to school. And it used to hurt me so bad that to see this man I used to work for; he had three kids, and I used to see his kids go to school. Bus used to come pick his kids up, take them to school, bring them home. I had to work in his field, and his son was almost my, around my age. And they was going to school when I had to go to work in this field. And I couldn't go to school. And that used to make me feel so bad, but there was nothing I could do about it. And it was a really rough time, you know, for me and my family. So I had to work.

Like Chief, George grew up on a sharecropper's farm in the 1950s. As the oldest son, he had to help support the family. Access to school was similarly limited by the demands of farm work; however, while Chief remembers school as a place where he wished he could spend more time, George recalls it as "terrible." On the occasions when he did go, he (also like Chief) had to walk about two miles each way. Once he arrived, George and the other boys were required to haul and chop wood to heat the building. Under those conditions, George insists,

School wasn't really, then, uh, you know, like when you go once or twice a week, you don't learn nothing, you can't learn nothing in that knowing two days, if you go two days, you know. So, it was really hard; I didn't learn nothing.

I had to work. I had no choice. I had to work to live and eat, have a place to live, so I did what I had to do. . . . I didn't know, I couldn't, I really couldn't even read my own name 'cause I didn't even go to school long enough to learn it. I'm telling you, I didn't know how to spell my name because schooling was something that I wasn't there long enough to learn. Then the little money that we make, we had so far to go on a little money. At that time they had no lunch at school, you know. And, um, when you go to school, if you do go, when you get there you be so *hungry* at lunchtime. You know, you ain't had nothing to eat, you don't get nothing to eat until you back home. You know? It was terrible time. It was a rough time. Life was really, really terrible.

George has always been motivated primarily by work, as he explains, starting from the age of ten when he had a business raising and selling pigs. Gaining and maintaining employment was never a problem. When he was seventeen, George left the South. He wanted to get away from farming. He had relatives in New York City and was able to get a job as a chauffeur. After some time, he moved up to Springfield, married, and with his wife raised two sons, both of whom have college degrees and no longer live at home.

For nearly twenty years, George worked in drop-forging, a hot, heavy, and precise process of shaping metal.

[I worked at] Moore Drop Forge, making different things for airplanes, and Ford Motor Company, and Sears, wrenches and one type or another. Wasn't a whole lot—they didn't know I couldn't read and write. Far as, um, you see, you had to set up a job. . . . When you set up a job, you got to be, like, you got to set up by a thousand, ten thousand, fifteen or twenty thousand, or either half a inch, a inch, or whatever; you know, you got to be exactly right. But see, I learned this from working with people, you know, from experience. I learned 'cause when you couldn't read and write, you have to make sure you know, you keep, you see, what you see, you know, in your head. You got to know what you learn, what you see other people do. And *I learned.*

The tough part was figuring out how to calculate measurements when he didn't know how to use classroom tools like a compass and protractor or how to read a ruler. George had to create his own formulas that were correct and precise and that wouldn't expose a gap in his learning. He didn't want other people to think that he didn't know. George was on a team of three, creating templates for mass production. The work was constant and it was hot. The men on the crew depended on one another; no one could slip up.

You know hard work didn't bother me so, and that was a hard job. But I learn . . . how to do the job. You know, and it wasn't a whole lot of reading and writing in the job. It's most something like was math. You know. That's what you had to, you know, kind of deal with most of the—math. And I learned . . . I was, I tell you, out of three hundred people in my department, I was the second highest paid man. They post it on the board, you know. That made me feel good because a lot of people didn't know I, didn't know I couldn't read and write, and being one of the second highest paid man in the shop, you know, out of all those people, it made me feel good, and I felt to myself, like I had accomplished something, and I know how to do my job. You didn't have to tell me I know how to do it, you know what to do, so it made me feel good.

Three hundred men viewed him as an expert. They acknowledged that George had "accomplished something." He knew it by his high wages. He was valued and he valued himself. People at the "Drop Shop" didn't need to know that he couldn't read and write, and George was able to keep his nonliteracy covered up with his outstanding workplace performance. But George's prowess didn't last. Sometime in the mid-1980s, the work was outsourced overseas, and the forge closed. The sudden shutting down of the forge, and with it the end of long-term, steady employment, came as a shock.

And they closed it; everybody around there was hurting. Some guys was too old to get another job, and some of them, a lot of guys, was lucky to get another job, you know? And me, I didn't have no education or go get a better job than I had there. And I began to worry, and I began to think . . . I began to think about my education then. You know, what I didn't have, to deal with searching, getting another job. I knew I could get another job, but I wouldn't get a job that paying me like the job that I had. . . . I didn't know where to go to get a education. I knew I couldn't just go to a public school; they wouldn't accept me. I was too old for that. And it took me a while before I found out; I went and got another job, you know, working. It wasn't what I wanted, but I had to live, so I kept, I had, uhh, houses, one stuff or another, you know, mortgage to pay. . . . I've had to work, but I still, in the back of my mind, I still wanted a education.

Nonliteracy gnawed at George in a way it hadn't in years. It was harder to push to the back of his mind. He took a job at the gun factory down the road, where he could do the work he knew, but conditions weren't as good. At Smith & Wesson, they had one man doing the job of three. George talked about what the changes stirred up:

Once I leave this place and go to another job, now, the people on the, on this next job are going to want to know, well, can I? Can you run this machine? Do you know how to operate this machine? And now you going to need education for that because if you don't know how to read and write, you can't operate no machine. . . . Because you have to know how to read and write *before* you can learn how to operate a machine, you know what I mean? And all that come into play. You think of all that go through your head, you know, all kind of thing. But I was fortunate enough to have—, I got another job doing the same thing I was doing there [*at Moore*]. And, 'cause, uh, when I went to Smith & Wesson, applied for a job, they needed somebody like me. And I had a skill to do that kind of job, and they didn't have to train me because I already knew how to do it.

FROM THE WORKPLACE TO THE LITERACY CENTER

Disability is what finally ended work for George, Chief, and Lee Ann. ✓ *Is it a coincidence that each of them labored until his or her body was worn to injury? I think not. Their competent, able bodies were the most reliable means of being that they knew. The body is strong and capable, dependable and knowledgeable, until accident or injury alters it. What can one do when the laboring body becomes disabled? Although each tells a different story of events that brought them to Read/Write/Now, disability was what finally shifted conditions drastically enough to lead them to study. As Lee Ann recalls, she was going to get another job after she got laid off by the city, but she was swayed by her daughter's words:* "Ma, take a break." *Does exercising the right to literacy mean that it is accessible only as a break from work? Do people like George, Chief, and Lee Ann deserve to become more literate only when their bodies are no longer suitable for labor? Whose body is consigned to physical work and whose is toned for intellectual labor? Did they have other choices? Does Violeta, who is twenty years their junior, have different options?*

I toss these questions out without clear answers but with the hope that they will expose what George and his peers' experiences reveal again and again: that their bodies were marked by nonliteracy and that their decision to seek an education later in life is a radical move toward reconfiguring mind and body. When George states, "you have to know how to read and write *before* you can learn how to operate a machine," *he is commenting on more than his fear of being obsolete. His anxiety about not being able to learn a new machine shows that he was no longer able to hide behind the bravado he displayed at the forge. He accepted the job that he could do without any new training, but reluctantly, and he did it until his leg was damaged in a workplace accident. Once he had healed, he came to Read/Write/Now to begin a new career as an adult learner.*

CHURCH AS A SITE OF TURBULENT FLOW

The story that best exemplifies the turbulence of embodying nonliteracy occurs in a church. In the following narrative, we witness the conflicting discourses that Lee Ann grapples with as she tries to be a good person and a good Christian. I had asked her whether she received writing and reading instruction in other settings besides school. She said, yes, church. When I asked her more pointedly whether she uses writing and reading at church, she divulged this:

I'm not joining anything because I didn't, couldn't read. Like the choirs and stuff like that. I remember one time I went to this church. They, they made me cry for a week. I've never been so hurt in all my life because I couldn't read, right? I stepped down in faith, and I went to this church. . . .

[The choir director] tested my voice, and he, so he said, he put me on the man's side. All the women was over here, and all the men was over here. Okay? He put me over there. So what happened is, so, I think he wanted to discourage me going, didn't want me involved in the program. So what happened is, so, I, the two people I sat next to, one was Marty. I'll never forget . . . his name is Marty, and he was married. And the other one was engaged, on the other side of me. Right? And I told the two gentlemen, I said, "Look, I joined this, I can't read and write." I said, "I joined it." I said, "Could you please help me?" Well, they were Christians, and they were kind; and when one wasn't there, the other one was there. So they helped me, you know, sing up. I said, "I can't read the words, and I can't read the music. I am stepping out in faith." So both, it worked out pretty good. And I went up there, on top, and sang with everybody else.

I was up there singing with everybody else. Right? Well, the guy didn't like it that ran the show. . . . [He,] then he put me on the woman's side. And a lot of them woman . . . they had their nose so high up . . . [in] the sky that the altitude could freeze it. I went over to ask them [to] help. . . . And, and they wouldn't help me. So that didn't discourage me. I still was a fighter. I'm still [not] going to [*whacks her fist on the table*] let them push me around. . . .

Okay? This is what he said to me, and it crushed me like a bug. . . . He stood up like this [*she stands up*] and he said, "We don't want anybody else here." And the fact now, everybody in this place can read. Everybody else in this place read music *and* words. I am the only dummy sitting there couldn't read music or words. I stepped down in faith now, right? And then he said to me, he said, "We don't want anybody else here hanging on anybody else's coattails!"

Well, he crushed me like a bug 'cause boy did that hit home. I said I am glad that I sat in the first row in that church. I am glad I sat in that first row because I was crying like a baby and the tears dripping down my face, because that's what he said to me: "We don't want" . . . And I am handicapped, and you're damned right I need a crutch, but when I learn something I don't need the crutches. . . . My face was swollen. And one of my close friends said, "What happened to you? Your face!" My face swollen like I ate ten thousand oranges, you know, so I got hives and stuff. My face is swollen from church? I said, "You know, I'm sitting there and sitting," and I said, "I'm glad there's nobody behind see me pouring tears in the church" because I was embarrassed. As soon as he, as soon as the church left, I boogied out the side door because I didn't want nobody to see me crying like that. . . .

That was it for me. I left that place. I left after he said to me, up there, "We don't want nobody. Everybody got to hold their own. Nobody else hanging on anybody else's coattails." That was me, buddy. That was *me*. And I said, "That's all right. You hurt me, but you hurt the Christ that lives inside me."

THE RESPONSIBILITY OF REPRESENTATION

Lee Ann tells it—shouting, pounding the table—she tells it again, bits of the story flying around like shards that cut and sting: "He's dying now. That man is dying now." *DID YOU GET THAT? For weeks afterward, every time she sees me Lee Ann asks whether I have published the story in the newspaper.* "Can you believe that?! . . . Can you believe that happened in a* church?" "And he's dying now," . . . *and she's back in. Lee Ann's story becomes my story; I carry it now. At the time, I took it home, listened to the recording, transcribed it, analyzed it in my dissertation, and then later read it aloud at conferences and worked parts of it into academic articles. I have been listening to Lee Ann's choir narrative for nine years. By giving me the story of this* *experience that she claims was one of the most harrowing of her life, Lee Ann has passed on the responsibility of representation. YOU WANT TO KNOW WHY? WHY DO PEOPLE WANT TO WRITE AND READ DIFFERENTLY? THIS IS WHY. THIS IS WHAT I CARRY INSIDE ME, AND YOU WANTED IT, AND NOW YOU BEAR THE RESPONSIBILITY OF KNOWING. NOW YOU KNOW WHAT THE VIOLENCE OF LITERACY[3] FEELS LIKE. By sharing it with me, Lee Ann made her story public. She wanted people to know; she wanted the newspapers to know. This is what can happen in a church. The hypocrisy, the contradictions. YOU WANT TO TALK TO ME? TO KNOW ME? THEN TAKE THIS. Truly, Lee Ann may never be able to unburden herself of her terrible experiences. But as she states repeatedly, she is a fighter, and I am certain she will continue to resist and expose the truth of what she notices all her life.*

Less than a year later, Lee Ann had left the center after studying with another teacher who did not understand her needs as well as Carolyn, her original teacher. I don't know where Lee Ann is now, but I do know that she left me with the responsibility to tend her story. What does that mean for me as a literacy researcher and as the writer of this book? On the simplest level, it means a commitment to tell the truth of Lee Ann's experiences and those of her peers. On another level, it assigns me the task I said I wanted when I asked people to tell me about their literacy experiences: To investigate those stories and the injustices that underlie them, to do the work they could not do on their own because no one was listening to them. To value the knowledge that Lee Ann and others like her have, but that many other people don't know about.

Lee Ann's implied question, Did you get that?, echoes Royster's question to writing studies scholars about how to do the active listening that is required to adequately absorb and convey a narrative like Lee Ann's:

How can we teach, engage in research, write about, and talk across boundaries with others, instead of for, about, and around them? . . . We need to talk, yes, and to talk back, yes, but when do we listen? How do we listen? How do we demonstrate that we honor and respect the person talking and what that person is saying, or what the person might say if we valued someone other than ourselves having a turn to speak? How do we translate listening into language and action, into the creation of an appropriate response? How do we really "talk back" rather than talk also? (38)

Ratcliffe notes that in posing these questions Royster "demonstrates how two or more people may interact so as to approximate equal positioning" (128). Though I do not claim that Lee Ann and I have equal positioning, I agree with Ratcliffe's interpretation of how Royster's questions might ideally operate. Lee Ann takes control of the moment. She tells me what kind of audience she wants me to be. In this way, she claims agency in telling her story on her own terms.

I end this chapter with Lee Ann's choir narrative because it calls into question my position as listener. Her comments to me afterward when she asks whether I've published the narrative in the newspaper challenge my idea of audience, force me into a role in which I have to be active as listener and literacy worker, for that is what Lee Ann is demanding. She insists that the listener not only take her story seriously but also make it public, putting me in a position in which listening also means acting in the way Lee Ann wishes. In examining the ethical responsibility of the intellectual who represents, Spivak exposes the always tricky center, the delicacy of knowing when to yield and when to intervene because it will help another person's voice to be heard. At the tricky center, we find the turbulent flow of people's discourses, which is unquestionable in Lee Ann's testimony.

Lee Ann performs the turbulent flow that she experiences as someone who is trying to hold on to her dignity while also making moves to change her life. She wants to be part of the people, to "sing up." Listeners (first me and now you) have little choice but to take in how painful her situation is and how angry she becomes as she realizes that agents within institutions that promote themselves as supporting people like her may not necessarily uphold their principles. When Lee Ann tells me the story of the church choir, she is self-representing in a particular way because she wants me (a white person from the world of higher education) to represent her in certain terms. This is her intervention. This is her way of speaking back to power. By speaking to me, Lee Ann and her peers speak to us.

⁓

A few years later, I give a talk at my university on Lee Ann's literacy practices with her Walmart statement in its title: "'Walmart Was Going to Hire Me, but I Can't Read the Coupons': Adult Literacy Education and Critical Citizenry." During the Q&A, one of the faculty members in the audience asks whether Lee Ann is crazy, suggesting that her testimony might not be rational and therefore is invalid. But I believe the question of Lee Ann's sanity is one that could be directed at anyone. My response to the audience member: You don't know Lee Ann, but everyone in this room has known someone like her. She is not unfamiliar to anyone here. Lee Ann's way of communicating her experiences provides a voice that no one else can offer. In Lee Ann—in all four participants—we can hear the subaltern subject, but only when readers acknowledge the veracity of her story. Hers is the voice no one wishes to hear, and for that reason alone, it is a voice that can make us more aware of our own assumptions and biases surrounding literacy. This is Lee Ann's story, as she wants to represent herself to us. If we can't hear it, or dismiss it as crazy, we fail to listen.

⁓

Lee Ann's demand that we listen helps to clarify how the listener/ researcher's involvement is crucial for Lee Ann to make the intervention she wants within literate mainstream culture (as she perceives it). In Chapter 3, I continue to examine the four participants' efforts at self-representation as I create space for them to speak for themselves. But their self-representation is always mediated by my roles as listener, researcher, and writer. The participants have expectations of me too. They want my inquiry into and documentation of their experiences to provide them with something important, and they continue to articulate those expectations in the following pages. Their speaking out becomes more complex as other voices enter the conversation—those of their teachers, their peers, the founder and coordinator of the literacy center, and this researcher —and the picture of their experiences becomes fuller.

3

Contemplating Literacy: "A Door Now Open"

~

YOU MAKE A LEFT IN THE LIBRARY LOBBY onto a small corridor lined with bulletin boards on both sides and shelves for notebooks, supplies, and announcements. On the boards are listings for apartments and information about housing and health benefits. Across the hall, another bulletin board celebrates learners' achievements: "Congratulations! You met your goal!" Photocopies of driver's licenses, certificates and merits obtained at work, citizenship papers, and library cards are all on display. The space opens up. Tall bookcases function as walls separating the classrooms: two in the main area and another smaller one attached at the rear, and a computer room. In a lounge toward the front is a place to snack and read. People come in here to make photocopies and use the fridge. On the shelves are publications from the center, the annual anthology of all the learners' writing, and some special texts. Most inspiring: a four-volume set of booklets written by a former student that begins with her childhood in rural Korea and continues up to the moment she publishes her memoir.

~

American adult literacy programs were originally shaped by the Canadian community writing movement, which advocated for publishing writing produced by learners. Such programs are often situated in libraries, and it is part of the American Library Association's mission to promote literacy learning (by providing classroom space and access to materials) for the public, especially to under-served populations (Horning). In the United States, writing tutors involved in adult basic education (ABE) initiatives were generally informed by Freire's work. Based on these influences, the Read/Write/Now Adult Learning Center has always had a liberatory philosophy that focuses on learners' writing. The center's founder, Marilyn Gillespie, created the program with the belief that writing enables adults to express ideas, solve problems, and respond to events in their environment. Writing is a daily part of learning and a central component of literacy education (Read/Write/Now, *My Life*).[1] Gillespie opened Read/Write/Now in 1987 "as a field site to test a computer-based curriculum for adults who read below a 'six grade' level" ("Becoming Authors" 60). Although the program has changed a lot since its early years, it has always valued writing as central to the curriculum (60–64).

Long after my project ended, I would meet Gillespie and wish that I had known her sooner. We would talk all night and into the morning. Over dinner, she told me about her job in a refugee camp in Thailand in the early 1980s where fellow teachers introduced her to Freire's work. Inspired by what she had learned in Thailand, she returned to the United States to study with Freire and get her PhD. During one of the summer sessions led by Freire and Miles Horton (of the Highlander Folk School), Gillespie had an opportunity to speak with Horton about her own ambitions. Her task, he told her, would be to start an adult literacy program based on Freire's principles.

Although this book is set at the Read/Write/Now Adult Learning Center, its focus is not on the center. Many writing studies investigate the site of literacy learning; that is not my concern. What is important in this book are the people who attend Read/Write/Now and how they represent literacy.

∽

Everybody at Read/Write/Now has a story. There's Calvin, who has been in and out of the center since it opened. He still sounds out every word when he reads, tracing a line under the text with his leathery brown fingertip and attempting to make meaning. And Terrance, who seeks advice from the teachers about how to handle his divorce. Sometimes he tears up when he talks about how his wife abused him, but then his tears reveal another level of frustration and anger as he describes his meetings with the lawyer, who demands that he sign here and here. The lawyer won't explain what the documents mean. He won't read them aloud to Terrance. He talks to him like Terrance doesn't understand. "Just because you can't read doesn't mean that you don't know," *Terrance trembles when he says this.* "It's unjust! I'm like a blind man." *He explains that people manipulate you when you don't know how to read and write, and their actions can be* "very hurtful." *There are women who had babies when they were girls or who had to raise their mother's babies, women who have endured jail sentences, abuse, depression, diabetes. There's always poverty. This book is about the literacy experiences of four particular people who studied at Read/Write/Now, but it could have been about many other learners who went there because, despite the challenges of their lives, they had always wanted to read and write.*

Midmorning at Read/Write/Now: conversations from the three classrooms hover in the air; these are the sounds of students talking about language or math or what's in the news. Teachers' instructional urgings rise over the general hum but are punctuated by other voices, and in Melissa's room there is continual laughter. Melissa's class of "intermediate" readers and writers is where I will find Chief and George, but at first they and their teacher stand out as rowdy noise that emanates from one end of the common space. In Carolyn's "developing" readers and writers group, the tone is lower, more focused on composing sentences and independent reading. Taps and murmurs come from the small computer room in back as some learners attempt keyboarding; none of them has ever typed before in a job or school setting. They navigate computers, figuring out what it means to create a document and save it. It will be some time before they are composing and revising on these machines.

I sit at the table among the class of developing readers and writers: Violeta, Calvin, Lee Ann, Terrance, and numerous others who come and go, some stopping out because of work or child care, some disappearing without an explanation, but most of the learners eager to be present in this moment around this table. A wire rack of paperbacks stands in a corner of the classroom space, and sometimes Carolyn will instruct her learners to grab a book or to finish what they are reading. The books look like early readers except that the content is geared to adult situations: employment, relationships, renting an apartment. Violeta reads quietly, seriously. Across the table, Lee Ann's attention is divided; she reads to herself, she reads aloud. She talks at the person next to her, interrupting his moment of solitude, and occasionally Carolyn has to remind Lee Ann, with a whisper or light tap on her shoulder, what it means to read silently. When it is writing time, Carolyn sets them up with the props they need: pencils, notebooks, and spelling dictionaries. The writing assignments go slowly as learners consult their lists of spelling words and concentrate on where to capitalize and where to leave a space. Carolyn presents simple lessons on word families and asks the students to sound out words; and they do, speaking aloud around the table, concentrating on getting it right, the stigma of their nonliteracy suspended when they are in class together.

For a while, I observe only Carolyn's classes and students, until I am drawn down the corridor by lively banter at the front of the center. There, Melissa sits on one side of a square of tables, facing her class of intermediate readers and writers.[2] This is the place to be, where learners are confident enough to make noise and tell jokes. Discussions of current events are raucous; math lessons are about whole-class participation; even grammar exercises turn into sessions of giving and taking it. Chief and George play off each other in a comedic duet, rolling out their remarks and cracking up. They have both lived a long time up north in Springfield and yet they can slide back into the cadence of the South; they can poke fun at each other and their teacher. Still, both men take their classwork seriously. They model for other (often younger) students that learning can be entertaining, that class is a place where they can play with ideas and have strong voices. Melissa draws them out with her high-involvement style of teaching. She is a grand presence herself, loud and inviting everyone to join in. And Chief is her best student, always respectful but so clearly having a good time—Chief, who admits now that he loves history, he loves learning; he will be studying for the rest of his life.

～

MUTUAL CONTEMPLATION BETWEEN PARTICIPANTS AND RESEARCHER

The act of listening can be approached from various positions. Royster and Kirsch propose a model for inquiry that they term *strategic contemplation,* which depends on the researcher's commitment to a meditative, introspective practice, suggesting "that researchers might linger deliberately inside of their research tasks as they investigate their topics and sources—" (84). Taking time for contemplation and recognizing such reflection as essential to the research process makes analysis more careful and multitextured. Royster and Kirsch tell us that being present in the moment influences the whole research process. Capturing the moment, being fully open to it during the research period and willing to contemplate the moment over time—over years—deepens our interpretations and provides new meanings for our work. It gives the research its vitality. Royster and Kirsch explain:

> This process of paying attention, of being mindful, of attending to the subtle, intuitive, not-so-obvious parts of research has the capacity to yield rich rewards. It allows scholars to observe and notice, to listen to and to hear voices often neglected or silenced, and to notice more overtly their own responses to what they are seeing, reading, reflecting on, and encountering during their research processes. Strategic contemplation asks us to take as much into account as possible but to withhold judgment for a time and resist coming to closure too soon in order to make the time to invite creativity, wonder, and inspiration into the research process. (85)

Strategic contemplation, as Royster and Kirsch define it, focuses on the researcher's mindful awareness. But I would argue that this practice is not merely about the researcher. It is also about the participants who engage in the strategic contemplation of literacy—what it means and what it does. I extend Royster and Kirsch's description of the researcher "linger[ing] deliberately" to include my participants in the process. In my case, the four participants lingered along with me. Their interviews (and subsequent informal conversations) relied on lingering in the moment together and contemplating their representation of their experiences as *mutual* contemplation. Throughout these chapters—and especially here in Chapter 3—the four participants are strategically contemplating literacy as a process of becoming. In their conversations with me, they are defining literacy as they see it based on their interpretations and reflections. All of us are literacy researchers together.

In this chapter, I look with the four participants as they contemplate their own literacy. I continue to frame a space in which their discourses "wash over, through and around" readers (Ratcliffe). My primary concern remains with presenting their voices in their own words without appropriating them; yet I am also present. This chapter is a conversation with multiple voices. In addition to the four participants who are now clearly situated at Read/Write/Now, other perspectives can be found here, including my own views of what it means to experience the narratives, to be an ethical researcher, and to reflect on how their ongoing desire for literacy shapes adult learners' experiences.

~

Violeta

On my first day in her classroom, I notice Violeta looking at me every time I glance in her direction; I cannot tell whether I am making her uncomfortable with my presence or whether she is interested in the stranger in the room. She says she wants to show me the portfolio of her work. Everyone at Read/Write/Now has a binder on the shelf that contains completed writing, but not everyone references the portfolio as Violeta does when she pulls it down that day: "This is my life book." *Her nod instructs me to start reading. She watches me thumb through the pages of the binder. When I linger on the confessional piece titled* "My Mask," *she says,* "That one I put in the publication anonymously." *I wonder: If she has published the narrative anonymously, then why is she willing to share it with a stranger? Why is she so trusting? Her dark, concerned eyes tell a different story from her open face and smile. Perhaps she believes her writing needs to be made more public. Is the writing in this portfolio her form of social action? Months later, I ask Violeta about her decision to share her personal writing with me so soon after we met. She is unruffled:* "And when I share you with this, I can feel it in my heart you a nice person. I know you no do with that. I can feel in my heart." *Although her life is difficult and complicated, Violeta is not cynical. She wants to be open to people, to learning, and to all life's experiences.*

Occasionally she brings her portfolio home to share with her children. Here's what Mami is learning in "school." *Each piece of her finished work is neatly preserved with a plastic cover, and each piece is accompanied by a written explanation of why she included it in the portfolio. Although this is the procedure that all learners are asked to use, only Violeta composes her book with such dedication. Only Violeta connects the portfolio to her life outside the program. Every narrative represents an aspect of Violeta's life and an opportunity for her to reflect on where she is in terms of the "progress" of her literacy education. What's inside her "life book"? Poems, stories, essays, and the periodic goal statements that everyone at Read/Write/Now is asked to write. This is where learners articulate their learning and life ambitions. For example, George wants to build a shed. Violeta wants to write a letter. She writes a letter to her son in prison. Then she writes a letter to her social worker. Violeta explains why in her monthly written goal statement:*

> My most important goal is to learn how to write a letter. I am going to start by learning how to make the letter. I will learn how to do the punctuation. When I do the letter I am going to use the words correctly in the present or past tense. I am going to write a letters to my son and my mother. When I am done with my letter, I am going to have my teacher check them.
>
> Writing a letter is important to me because I want to write a letter. I never wrote a letter by myself. I would like to do a letter by myself. When some people write a letter to me, I want to write back but I don't know how to write a letter. This is important for my life.

While Violeta's classmates edit and type their goal statements, she moves ahead and composes her first letter. Violeta says that she spoke with her son on the phone the night before. Then why write a letter? Why not just talk? "Uh-uh," she explains carefully, shaking her head so I will get it: the phone conversations are in Spanish, but the letter is going to be in English. She wants to write the letter to justify why she reported her son to the police when she discovered that he was using and selling drugs. She did this to get him off the streets so he would not get killed.

Dear Miguel,

The reason I am writing this letter is because I love you very much. Please don't get in trouble any more. Remember God is all the time with you. I know you are now in the wrong place. You didn't do the right thing. My dear son, I

think about you all the time. I hope you have learned the
right way now.
    I am going to P.R. this summer. I would like to see you
doing excellent in your life. Remember you have children.
When your children ask about your life, what answer are you
going to have for you children? I will feel better if you try to
do something nice in your life. When you do the right thing
you will feel proud.
    This is my little letter for you. I hope when you get this
letter you feel good. God bless you.

Love,
Mom

*Violeta says there's something about writing a letter that she cannot
achieve by talking on the phone. In the letter, she gets to have her say.
She gets to make her words permanent, and maybe her son will want
to reflect on what she says. Maybe she can defend her position, and he
will not be angry with her for turning him in. Her comments suggest
that she contemplates how writing can offer her something different
from speech. She has control over her language, and her son will not
talk back. Violeta can express herself more effectively in English than in
Spanish. I notice the difference between her comments in English and
the voice in her writing as we discuss her literacy. In speech, Violeta's
English falters. She uses Spanglish. But in writing, she is able to craft
her words. Her remarks about her "life book" help me to understand
why Violeta values herself as a writer and why she prefers to write a
letter to her son rather than call him.*

    *Most of the writing in Violeta's portfolio is autobiographical, reflec-
tive poems and short essays; but her writing is changing. Her early work
followed the themes and formats suggested by her teachers, yet even with
the letter to her son she was already explaining that she was deciding
to do something different—to claim writing for her own purposes. In
contrast, here is an early poem that was a class assignment:*

I Am From

I am from Puerto Rico and New York too,
fruit trees, beaches, lakes, farm animals, big
buildings, school, laundromats, and farmers' market.

I am from flying kites, shooting marbles with friends,
jumping rope, weekends at my "abuela's" house,
fishing, shrimping and catching crabs with my family.

I am from "pasteles", "arroz con gandules," "funche con
pescado," "arroz con dulce," "bianda" and "bacalao."

I am from my mother saying "Don't go to the beach by
yourself" and "Put your shoes on," and my sister
saying, "Leave me alone." The sound of the garbage
truck said my father was here.

I am from my "abuela's" figurines, my mother's
romantic music and "morenga", my "abuelo's" TV
program and lunchtime and my great-grandmother's
picture.

I am from my mother and father, abuelo and abuela,
my uncle and aunt, sisters, brothers, cousins and
my stepmother and stepfather.

*The poem follows a format, and it adds up to a pleasant recollection
of a charming childhood in Puerto Rico. But a year later, Violeta wrote
a very different narrative for a program-wide publication on domestic
violence. She had started to use writing to examine her relationship to
family and society.*

I Know How It Feels

Since I was 9 years old, I grew up in an abusive family. I was the oldest. My mother never sent me to school so
I could help her raise my 5 brothers and my 4 sisters. After
my mother and my father separated, my mother got another
husband who was a drug dealer. He used to hit my mother
and used drugs in front my brother and me and my sisters.

In my young life I saw a lot of drugs and physical abuse
and never got support from my mother. Up to this day, I
never tried to use drugs or drink. And now I got the opportunity to go to school and be somebody in the future.

*Violeta states that there are many reasons why writing matters.
Some of her intention is functional:*

When I have to sign form or when I sign my paper for Section 8, before I was no doing that. Now I sit down, and I read it, and I sign it. I no was doing that before. Like my paper for Section 8, it was a lot of paper. Before I was going crazy. I had to get it from help. I do that now with myself.

Her comments point to a strong wish to take care of herself and her children so that she can be independent and in greater control of her life. Never does she claim to want a boyfriend or a husband or more money in order to improve conditions. She always talks about becoming stronger, more independent, more capable, more educated, a better learner, a more knowledgeable parent, and a woman who can be strong for other women. Violeta's conversations with me about "keep[ing] it moving" through her life and using her literacy to become a stronger woman show me that she does not dream of a traditional family structure. At times in her life, she has been overpowered by men, by the effects of other people's control and lack of control, by poverty, and by ill health. What she wants now, as I understand it from listening to her, is personal strength and the ability to share what she knows with others.

By the time I met her, Violeta already spoke of writing as a means of becoming, my word but her concept, a theory without the theoretical language. Most of her comments about writing connect the process with working out the story of her life. We talked about that relationship:

What do you like to write?"
About my life. About my life, yeah.
So when you do the kind of projects that Carolyn has you doing here, are those enjoyable to you?
Mm hmm. I do, partly, part of my portfolio is about my life. That's what I do. Because that helping me a lot to get out what did I go in and explain to me. And I do about my life book. I want to see when I before, was Violeta before? Was Violeta right now? The progress that I make.
So you want to look at your progress?
Mm hmm.
Is it special to you to get down those stories too?

Is special for me. *Porque* I can see the difference. I can, when I do that, when I was writing about my life, I can see I was afraid before. I not right now. I can see the progress. I was before afraid [to] get out [in] front of the world. Before I would say, "I cannot do this. This is not for me. Uh-uh." I don't know how to get it, *pero* when I get any and open the door for me and I do it, I can see the difference about my life.

Violeta continually refers to education as a "door open." Before, the door was closed, and even though she knew what lay behind it, literacy was unattainable. She was locked inside, the door sealed between her and both street and school, preventing her from having the freedom to pursue anything more than domestic responsibilities. Now Violeta raises her own children and also cares for her daughter's babies. She worries about the children of her son in prison. She worries about her own compromised health. But she also finds time to acknowledge that there is a "door now open"[3] and that she can slip through that door to give herself the literacy education she has wanted all her life. There is nothing specific that she wants from literacy, but Violeta's discussion makes it clear that she has begun a process she wants to "keep moving."

Lee Ann

She asks me why I am there. I am trying to keep my presence small, to observe and interact a bit but without taking on an active role as a teacher or volunteer. Sitting back and just taking things in as an academic researcher is new for me, and I am unsure how well I will be able to listen without participating. I explain that I am doing research on why people want to write and read. Lee Ann gives it back to me: "I want to read the instructions on the Hamburger Helper." *At first I think she is talking about functional literacy: she wants to be a more competent cook and shopper. But I am wrong; I am misreading Lee Ann by making this assumption. As I get to know her, she helps me to understand that she wants to break free of a sense of entrapment; she wants something else.*

Why do you want to write and read differently?

Well, like I say, all my life people had to help me. I can't write a letter. My son got in trouble and, ahh, and he's begging for me to write, to have somebody help me write him a letter. And my mail gets piled up and piled up with boxes because I have to wait 'til my daughter or somebody comes because I can't read all the, my mail and letters and different things people send me, you know, contests, anything. It's hard. And labels, especially labels on food, it's hard to read labels on food. You know . . . I've never learned how to write a letter, you know, I'm older now. Write a letter to my kids and son and stuff. So, and this is the closest now. This year I think is going to be my year.

At Read/Write/Now, Lee Ann writes "independently," which means that she composes on her own without a teacher recording for her or spelling out each word. She is partial to skills exercises and seems to enjoy reviewing rules, such as "silent e," or learning families of words. She says she likes the math instruction. She likes accounting. But writing remains difficult, not the content but the mechanics, like how to combine letters into words. Lee Ann is conscious of the acts of decoding and composing and worries over every word. None of it is second nature. She asks a lot of questions about word order, word choice, and especially spelling.

One day while I am observing, Lee Ann and her classmate Terrance wrestle with a writing assignment. They both ask me for assistance to the point that each becomes annoyed when I give attention to the other. Lee Ann finally bursts out that writing is too hard, she can't do it; she storms out of the classroom and out of the building. Terrance remains in the room, worn and quiet. But before long Lee Ann returns, and then she is able to talk with Terrance and me about the frustration they both experience when writing. It's not like reading, which unlocks culture and offers itself up to them. Writing is about too many rules. It brings back their earlier failures and blocks, reminds them of feeling unable.

I think of Lee Ann at home in her kitchen, showing me the letter magnets on her refrigerator, which she has attempted to form into the "five wh's" in a list (who, what, where, when, and why), but not all of the "wh" words are correct. This is a self-imposed task, not an assign-

ment she would get at Read/Write/Now. I wonder why she has set up this exercise for herself, and then Lee Ann tells me: this display is her effort at "getting it." As I listen to her explain her reasons for displaying and memorizing the "wh's," *I start to understand her rationale: practicing a conventional act of literacy acquisition will give her the winning ticket, the way in to acquiring standard spelling.*

Carolyn

Carolyn had worked at the center for more than eleven years when I first came to Read/Write/Now and would be there another two before she left to teach ABE at the nearby men's prison. She had a way that encouraged and supported the developing readers and writers she worked with at Read/Write/Now. While the energy in her classroom was often frenetic as learners struggled to compose, disrupting one another and continually consulting the spelling dictionaries beside them on the table, Carolyn was steadying. She reviewed skills exercises slowly and broke lessons down into manageable increments. She kept an eye on everyone. Carolyn explains her approach to teaching writing:

Students come in wanting to write their life story. . . . Or write a résumé. Or write a letter. They set goals in writing for themselves. And we're pretty flexible in terms of, like, I'm not preparing them to take a GED, so I'm not working on essay writing. . . . My goal maybe is just to have them write a paragraph, um, or address their goals. If they come in saying, "I really want to write a letter to my son because he's away or he's in jail," that's my goal. We work on that. . . . I try to include the skill building in whatever piece of writing they choose to work on. Sometimes they come to me saying, "I don't know what to write today," and I'll throw out an idea or give them a topic to write on. But a lot of times it's "What do you want to write? What is your goal for writing? What is it that you want to be able to do as a writer that you can't do and need some help with? And that's the program philosophy too, to meet their goals as learners, as family members, as community members, you know. What is it that you need to do? "Oh, I have to write a letter to my child's teacher." . . . And learners hear what other learners want to write, and they say, "Yeah, I want to be able to do that too." So, before you know it, you have five out of eight people with the same writing goal. And you say, "Let's make this a writing lesson." You know, let's work on it together as a group.

Carolyn and Melissa were my guides. They could explain every policy from Department of Education mandates to the intake exams they used to assess new learners. They knew where to get help for domestic violence, housing problems, substance abuse, free legal advice, everything. The teachers kept bus tokens in a drawer to dispense to anyone who needed fare. And they could read their students so well. Carolyn and Melissa helped me to choose the four learners who became the participants in my study. They knew who was reliable and who would want to talk. They provided the information and insight that allowed me a way in.

Not every teacher wants to work with adult learners. I have watched some teachers at Read/Write/Now collide with their own limitations. If you buy into the idea of a meritocracy that rewards some people because they earned it—and on the flip side fails others who somehow deserve to be denied literacy—then you don't want to teach adult learners. They'll call you out on it too. If there's one thing this population notices, it's when they're being condescended to. Adult learners already understand Graff's literacy myth (Literacy Myth, "Nineteenth-Century Origins") and how the falsity operates, how it maintains a society in which literacy can be withheld from some citizens. It reminds them too much of past pain, and they don't want to reexperience it with their Read/Write/Now teachers. They've already had those teachers and the rejection they associate with them. They resist the teacher who brags about the reading achievements of her ten-year-old, who has already surpassed them. However, the teachers who are committed to this population get something special that they can't get from other students. Carolyn started out in elementary education but then shifted over:

Well, I tried my hand at doing the kid thing. I realized I wasn't so great at it, and I still wanted to teach. I really felt I could be an effective, good teacher. And I found a very receptive audience in adult education. They are so . . . for the most part they are just so motivated. They just so want to be here. They're so interested in learning. That whole discipline factor thing is not a problem, and

I just, I found the right element for me to do what I want to do, which is teach, and do it to a group of people who want to learn. You know, what could be better!

Chief

Everyone at Read/Write/Now knows Chief. Certificates of his achievements are posted publicly on the bulletin boards: certificate to perform small engine repairs; certificate to drive a school bus. Although he is older than many of his peers and sometimes shuffles his feet, he more often moves with the relaxed gait of someone who has engaged with life for a good many years. Chief laughs a lot, a low tone, and his words roll around in his mouth like marbles. Something of a smile spreads across the lower part of his face and jaw, as if he is enjoying a joke that he chooses to keep to himself. Sometimes Chief appears sleepy. Sometimes he wears a tracksuit and a towel around his neck. He comes to class prepared to work and to engage, and he does just that.

Chief writes himself inspirational notes. They are tucked into his ✓ *portfolio between the goal statements and the editor's letters he used to publish in the* Read/Write/Now Daily News. *This one is from his early years in the program:*

Dear Chief
I am writing to tell you how proud I am of the work you have done this year at R-W-N. Some of the thing you should be most proud about are that you have learn to read and understand what you are reading. I am glad you are enjoying it. I'm proud that you have read eleven books. A couple of your most important stories are on Black History Month about Dr. Martin Luther King and Malcolm X.

I understand you like your teachers here at R-W-N. You like working with the Monthly News. And you like working with your good friends. I hope in the next year you continue to read and write more. I am proud to see you have done well. I like the two stories you wrote about Dr. M.L.K. Jr. and Malcolm X.

Keep up the good work
Chief

Now Chief can be his own good father, giving himself the nurturance he suggests he wishes he had had as a boy. Chief can also be his own good teacher, assessing himself at the end of the school year: I am proud of you, Chief. *Encouraging himself, celebrating his reading, his writing, especially when it's on history and race, and his leadership as editor.* "I am glad you are enjoying it," *Chief tells himself, because now he finally gets to have what he has always wanted. He savors it; he acknowledges the joy he gains and not just that reading and writing will qualify him for a better job someday. Literacy is not just fodder for employment. Although he is the first to admit—often with sadness— that he could have gone much further than he did in the workforce if he had been more literate, he also is aware that literacy carries much more value than credentials for work. Chief is very clear about the multiple purposes of literacy in his life. When we talk together, Chief's remarks make me realize that he has contemplated his desire for literacy throughout his life and that he sees the processes of reading and writing as multifaceted.*

Before I knew him and the program, Read/Write/Now established an inhouse newsletter, and Chief was its original editor. He explains that the paper got started because he and a classmate had an idea and the support of a teacher who helped them write and lay out the paper on the computer:

When we first started that, we had a lot of peoples interested in writing. In writing, uh, uh, what we call "getting the scoop." . . . The students would go and get news. Helping us with the news. And we would put it together. Me and, uh, Peters . . . me and him was the founders of the paper.

Here is one of Chief's editor's letters:

To my dear student and friends
As you know we almost didn,t have a pape last month. So I would like to encourage you to write more. We have a lot of people reading our pape. We have peope in Allen Town Pennsyl Vanial. And I also take them to my church and menbers-all ask me when is your next pape coming out. They say they really enjoy reading what the students write about. So

students,lets get the ball rolling. We lik to thank out president of R/w/n Daily news,Ellen, for list month's edition.
Chief Editer.

Although Chief's editing skills were rough at the time of this editor's letter, in conversations with him it is clear that being editor was personally beneficial because he could motivate himself to develop his writing, that he enjoys interacting with others, and that he views himself as a leader who can give advice. The inhouse newsletter offers Chief a forum for expressing his ideas where he won't be judged for his grammar errors. Since he is addressing other learners like himself, he doesn't have to feel self-conscious about mistakes. Chief's comments about his work as editor are a continual reminder of the many purposes literacy serves for him. Foremost, he explains how important it is to reach out to people and share his ideas so that he can make others think about the issues he has been contemplating.

Who is reading the paper in Allentown, Pennsylvania? Chief laughs when I ask him. He has a sister who lives there. He had been distributing the paper in his church, and then he sent copies to his sister to hand out at her church. He wants people to read his writing. The newsletter will get more people interested in reading and writing. Now that he has become more literate, Chief seems to feel responsible for pushing other people to think as hard as he does. He wants everyone to be interested in what he finds important. He writes (and he speaks about writing) as someone who wants to make people question things, who will use writing to have an effect and get things done. He admits that he sees himself as someone who can "speak to the peoples and get their attention and, I know what they need. Because, like I said, I have been down the road. I know what it's like."

When he was editor, Chief stayed late in the afternoons to edit the paper. He wanted to get everyone talking, not only at his church and his sister's church but also at Read/Write/Now. He understood that his ideas had validity and that he could use writing to create a public voice. For example, Chief wrote an advice column called "He Said/She Said." This article is from his second year in the program:

To He Said And She Said
This is your Editor Chief Dawson I am not a marriage counelor. But my wife and I live together for about three or four yeas before we got marrid. And yes The Bible speaks against it. But there are a lot of peoples doing it my wife and I have been married for nineteen years and I love it. A married is what you make of it two people have to work together.

Chief's goal is to assert his ideas even when they challenge the Bible. People should listen to him because he is an expert, as editor and as someone who has experienced life. From this position, he can use writing to encourage readers to consider that it is more important for two people to "have to work together" than it is to always follow the word of the Bible. Polished writing is not what Chief is after; his purpose is to speak to the people.

What does Chief use writing for outside of Read/Write/Now? We talk about practical household types of writing:

Well, I've come a long way on my writing. Now I can write checks. And that's what something that my wife, I am pretty sure, she glad of that.

Because she did all the bills before?

Yes, and now I got to where I can do the bills and help her to have a, the bills and take care of writing checks, balance the check books. That's something that I'm very proud of.

What about things like, um, church? Do you do any writing or reading, reading in church?

Yeah, well, I read the Bible in church along with the congregation. I am on the Trustee Board, and I am a president of the choir. . . . I sing with the choir as well as also direct it, which I am not very good at, but that's where they put me at. I do the best I can.

And, uh, do you use writing for things like going to the supermarket, writing lists? Well, you said paying bills. Phone messages or memos, any notes around the house?

I leave messages for my wife sometime, but, ahh, she does the grocery shopping. So, that's, uhh. I don't do none of that.

Chief is typical of men of his generation who have left the literate activities of household management to their wives. Because his wife (like his sisters when he was growing up) was the more literate of the couple, she took on the responsibilities of bill paying, grocery list making and shopping, and all of the written correspondence, such as writing notes to children's teachers and letters to relatives. I have learned from talking with learners at Read/Write/Now that the balance of responsibilities tips when the less literate partner becomes more able to participate in household literacy activities. For Chief that doesn't mean much of a change beyond helping his wife out a bit more, but for other learners in less traditional or stable relationships, the shift in one person's literacy can cause upheaval. A few of the men at the center speak of the disruption in their relationships when they start to write checks and pay bills. It takes some of the control away from their female partners. They argue and have problems they didn't have before when one person had control of all the financial tasks. Decision making changes and some relationships end.

I go to Chief's house once more, this time with Melissa. We are there to visit and bring a gift because Chief has had a stroke. Since his wife works with geriatric patients and she diagnosed him right away, Chief is going to be fine. Still, he moves slowly, and his words are more garbled, as though now there really are too many marbles in his mouth. He loves the large history book Melissa picked out, says he's going to read it soon. After he recovers, Chief will start a new job driving a minibus of older people around the city. He likes this work. It is better than when he drove kids, who made too much noise. His time at Read/Write/Now ends for now, but Chief visits. He is not breaking any ties. One day, he says, he may want to write a book about his life. He reflects on the possibility: "There's a lot of stuff in my life that I'd be able, that I might could put in a book." *Maybe one day he will take his GED and then go to community college, as he says he will. This is his hope:*

I would like to—in fact, when I finish Read/Write/Now and get enough—maybe I can go to college. Because the way I feel now, I would never quit-start school. No. I'll probably be going 'til, 'til I die. But hey, the more you learn, the more you crave for it. I don't know. I missed so much not being able to read. And now I'm reading and I see what I missed, and I just want to learn more.

George

"Are we guinea pigs?"

I've just given a simple explanation of who I am and why I'm there, but George rebuts my introduction to his class. I argue a weak "no," *(Melissa looks at me quizzically, as if to ask, how are you going to respond to that one?), but George's remark has already said it: I don't believe you, white lady.*

George, the most outwardly sociable and yet in some ways the most inhibited of the four participants I worked with, sometimes seems to be approachable, but other times he retreats. He always looks fine, nicely dressed and aware of the presentation he is making. Good student and bad boy at once, challenging Melissa on everything, though some of his overt behaviors belie his urge to understand whatever she can offer him: "Melissa, explain this to me . . ."; "Melissa, that makes no sense." *When Chief is there, George is balanced by his classmate's sincerity and warm humor. Though not exactly friends, they share experiences and a way of interacting in the classroom, and whereas Chief soaks up every bit of every lesson, George wrings it back out. He challenges, disrupts, cracks up, and pokes fun at his classmates (especially the women); but his probing questions are real ones and are sometimes hard to answer. At break time, he is out in the parking lot with the men. Most of them are smoking (not George) and talking loudly in a clump near their trucks. George drives a full-size pickup (neatly waxed) that is parked among his peers' all in a line in the front row closest to the building. George and the other African American men of his age cluster between their vehicles and the library entrance. He likes to hold the floor:* "The way I see it . . . I'm telling you . . . Let me explain something . . ." *followed by a laugh, a joke, a story about common hard times, truck engines, home repairs, building projects. Until it's time to go back inside and concentrate on "school" and the still daunting work of literacy learning.*

When I approached the people I hoped to work with as case study participants, the two women responded immediately with excitement, asking when we would begin. Chief, though less enthusiastic initially, said okay, it would be fine. But George, who I assumed would be willing, even forthcoming, would not make eye contact. What would he have to do, he wanted to know?

Meet with me to talk about your writing.

Are you going to take pictures?

No, I'm just going to talk with you, no pictures. And, I'm going to make a copy of all your writing.

It's not any good.

It doesn't have to be good. I'm just going to talk to you about your writing.

I'll have to think about it. I'll let you know.

How could this be? George's reluctance forced me to confront myself—white, younger, literate, female—and guess at how he might rank these categories. I figured that literate trumped the others, but I worried over the way I was presenting myself to him. When I spoke with Pamela, the program coordinator, she told me it was none of that. George doesn't want his picture taken. He doesn't want people to see that he goes to a literacy center. He is afraid of being evaluated. It had taken him years to trust Melissa and her. And you should see how he used to resist writing. For his first few years in the program, George wouldn't write anything. Melissa was adamant that it would be good for him to have to discuss his writing with me. So she spoke with George, he said yes, and we moved ahead, but cautiously. I was so careful preparing for George's interview and interacting with him at the center. I wanted to do all the right things to show I was an ethical researcher who respected him. Over time I would come to understand that his frequent displays of reluctance were a performance; that he was, in fact, preoccupied with how he would appear in public,[4] *as Pamela had claimed. But at that moment, I tried to compensate for his unwillingness, as well as my own anxiety that he would show up at the interview and refuse to speak, by completely rewriting my questions to suit him. I softened them. "How can I draw him out so he won't quit?" I asked myself again and again as I prepared for our meeting.*

We are alone in the library. George asks me whether I will be publishing the interview in the newspaper. No, I assure him, nothing in the news and no photos of him, ever. He likes going over the consent form; it relaxes him a bit. I ask the first questions: "Did you attend school? Where? When?" George launches into the entire story of his education, his lack of schooling, coping with nonliteracy throughout his life, his desire to get an education in recent years. He speaks with hardly a pause for one hour, and then, "Well, I guess I gotta go now," and we are done.

George's initial resistance to participating in my study, and his various performances of self-consciousness, taught me to interpret his experiences as an adult learner in a way that was different from what I had intended or expected. "Standing under" the words of all four people required rhetorical listening and continual willingness to make changes, to adjust research questions, and to question myself through strategic contemplation. I became able to (as Ratcliffe claims we can do with our university students) "listen to [a student's] listening" by being open to being changed by what I learned. George's interpretation of his experiences influenced my understanding of him, his peers, myself, and my own intent. His interpretation became our mutual contemplation.

Here's how George describes his shift from worker to student. After he retired on disability, George came to Read/Write/Now, but defining himself distinct from work was challenging. Even now he talks about education in economic terms.[5] We discuss his opinions on education during numerous interviews over a period of about five years. In this excerpt, George and I have been reviewing one of his interview transcripts. We each have a copy. Mine is marked up with questions and places that I want to call to his attention. George's copy is clean. He takes the transcript seriously, as though together we are examining a crucial document. He follows along when I point to areas where I have a question, running his finger across his own text. We are both literacy researchers working together.

Even with all the good money I was making, I really wanted to learn how to read and write because it didn't dawn on me that day was going to come when I was going to need it. [But] I wanted to know. Because I, even in my mind, I know if I knew how to read and write, even with the good money I was making, I could have done better, you know what I mean? . . .

Did it [literacy] seem like something you could ever have? I mean, did it? You know, it sounds like it sort of lurked in the back of your mind all the time, but it wasn't something you could get to because you were having to work all the time, and you knew how to work (and work well) and take care of your family. . . . But did, did it [education] seem like something you would ever get to have?

No. No, 'cause it looked, I was getting older. And life was beginning to look different. You know? It looked like it was out of reach, at the time. . . . There hadn't even never come a time I didn't even think about it [education] anymore because it didn't, it looked too far away, it looked, you know, beyond what I was going [to] get.

Uh huh. Did it seem okay to [you] as long as you were making a good living that it was out of reach?

No, it never was okay.

What does it mean to George to become more literate? He wants not to be embarrassed or shamed, as he explains in the opening of Chapter 1. He wants dignity. But when we talk about it, he explains that maybe he didn't know exactly what it was that he meant—or wanted—when he began to study at Read/Write/Now. As he has continued to study, literacy has taken on new meanings for George. But up until he came to the center, his primary lens for interpreting the world was through work and the self-sufficiency he could claim as a worker.

I only was taught to believe in work. Because if you work you can help yourself, you don't need nobody to help you. . . . You don't have to—I don't want to be paying nobody for anything, for nothing. I want to earn what I get. I don't want no handout. . . . I want to work for what I get, just pay me what I work for, not no more, I ain't asking no more, just pay me what I earn. That's—and I figure, if you do that, you can take care of yourself and take care of your family. You know?

Work demonstrates his competence and his worth, but George describes how he finds a certain kind of self-sufficiency in literacy too—not the same as the self-sufficiency he earns from work, but self-sufficiency of a different sort. Again, we talk about it while reading through his transcript from a previous interview:

Um, here you said: "All of my family is hardworking people."
Yep.

"And I love to work, too."

Yep, I do.

"But I also want to learn how to read and write so I could be self-sufficient." *In this story,*[6] *what does it mean to be self-sufficient?* Well, I tell you. When I say that word, it mean quite a few things. That don't mean one thing there, that mean quite a few things. It mean, I could go to the store and read whatever I buy, the label. Uh . . . I don't have to ask nobody if I can get on a road and read a sign and go wherever I want to go. I can pick up a book and read a book. Different things that a person with a education could do. That's what I mean. Not by no working because working, I always did that. That, that mean other things I'm talking about. Reading a book. Go read the Bible. Go to the store and buy something. Go pick up the can, or, or the box and read the label and see what in one, stuff or another. I can go pick up a newspaper and read the newspaper. Things like that, you know. And, um, and, you know, make out my own checks, write my own letter. You know? All kind of thing. That, that word, that word [*self-sufficiency*]—to me, mean a whole lot of thing.

I learn from George that he understands literacy *as having a broad meaning, and he sees the concept broaden the more literate he becomes. Literacy learning is different from other work he has done: you don't master a skill set like you do at a job. You read, and then you read more. You read what you want without having to get approval or be granted access. You can write if you need to write a check or if you want to write a letter. The self-sufficiency is expansive; a literate person can branch in many directions. The self-sufficiency that literacy allows is* "quite a few things," *the many ways George's mind can explore, and he can follow his mind's journey. Take, for example, his comments about China and Russia:*

Let's say you pick up a book over there, uh, you know, that, explaining something that happen in China. Russia. Someplace. Now, if you start reading that book and put your mind to that book and read what you, what that book is saying, now your whole thought and mind is over there. But you never been over there [never actually been to Russia or China] and you probably will never get there. But you could picture in your mind what you read, or, you know, what they saying. All the places, you know, what it's about. . . . And, so, I think . . . reading is, is, stimulates your mind, you know, it's just this—help you grow and, in a way, you know . . . and help you see things in your mind and in, things like ordinarily you wouldn't have. You couldn't read; you couldn't see that, you know, couldn't picture that picture in your mind.

The "school year" ends in the middle of summer with a publication, a reading, and a celebration. Everyone gathers in Melissa's classroom for the reading. Some learners stumble as they read aloud, others cry. For a few, it is the first time hearing their own voice reading, and maybe someone will remark on the strangeness of hearing yourself and knowing that those words in your ears are reading *and the thing you are reading is your own* writing. *The readers finish, and then there is a feast—every ethnicity of chicken, rice, beans, noodles, goat, pork, fish, salads, fruit—though nobody bakes. George brings his wife's famous macaroni and cheese. Melissa directs me toward it—"You want George's." He approaches me twice during the party, and I am surprised because George has previously averted his eyes and maintained some distance whenever we speak. But now George comes right to me. "Lauren," he announces, and it is the first time he has called me by name. He wants to talk about his last interview. It was a great experience. It makes you think about things that you might not otherwise think about, he says, things about your life. They might be things on your mind, but they're not things that people ask you about. They're things you want to talk about, things you may be thinking about that you want to tell people, but no one is going to ask. And it's really good when someone does ask to be able to talk about those things, to be able to think them through by talking about them with someone.*

Melissa

In Melissa's intermediate class, which so often sounded like a party, writing time was quiet. People were able to turn inward and focus without distraction, unlike in the developing readers and writers class, where learners constantly sought Carolyn's and their peers' assistance with writing tasks. Melissa guided her students, but she also knew when to leave them be. I ask Melissa: "How do you see the role of writing in people's lives?"

Well, if you ask anybody, "What kind of writing do you do in your life?," they'll say none . . . 'cause they don't think that like writing shopping lists and writing checks and writing messages and writing notes involves writing. . . . They just—it's at this point second nature to so many of them because they forgot where they were three years ago, or four years ago.

For instance, there's something George said in class just this morning—

It came totally out of nowhere. Well, he was looking at Connie's graham crackers, and he said, "Man, she paid too much money for those." I said, "I know." He's like: "She could have bought it in the regular store [instead of the health food store]." I said, "I know. Regular graham crackers don't have that much fat in it." And I think that's what . . . and then he stopped, and then all of a sudden—BOOM! This came out. Like Whoa! And for him, as you know, he wouldn't, and refused to write for many years. So, for him to just say, "Okay, I'm writing it now," is amazing. He was just like, "You know, I feel so good about being able to go in the grocery store and just read anything I want to read and look at the fat content and blah blah blah." He's like, "Man, I, sometimes I'll just go in the store and just read everything."

Like Carolyn, Melissa reflects on the joy of working with adult learners who want to learn and are clear about their motivations:

Each day is like a little present. Especially when you hear George, like that thing George said today. . . . Or just seeing the improvement that somebody makes. . . . Because it takes such courage for them to step in here that I can't imagine wanting to be any place else and wanting to be working with anybody, any other people who are so (I don't want to say "needy" 'cause I don't mean needy but) willing, wanting, I don't know . . . It's not for the money, I can tell you that! . . . I mean, there's not many jobs you can go to where people REALLY want what you have to give them.

Over the years, Melissa became my friend. This friendship included her contacting me if George was writing a new narrative that she knew I would want to come in to discuss with him, or if there was some intrigue at the center (e.g., invasive policies, trauma in someone's life). Conversations about our lives wove together with conversations about their lives: her students, my research participants, her job, my scholarship, our families, the center, the other teachers.

But things end in unexpected ways. When we reconnect after a couple of years out of contact, I learn that Melissa now lives in a different state and has broken off most of her ties to Read/Write/Now. The times of sitting together at the local Lebanese restaurant and talking endlessly about George and Chief are over for good. I realize that my research— like all research—is just about a moment (even if the moment lasts for years) when people came together in a place.[7]

~

I am aware of the impossibility of representation without some appropriation. The narratives I retell here, in spite of my best efforts at staying true to the speakers' intentions, must still reflect the goals of my research. The feminist scholarship on rhetorical listening and on strategic contemplation has provided me with the best guide I know for how to be introspective and self-interrogative when I am alone and how to listen carefully and engage in mutual contemplation when I am with the participants.

When I was collecting and analyzing data, I worried about whether I could get inside the participants' stories to capture their experiences fairly and ethically. Now I worry about removing myself enough to allow them to adequately represent themselves. I am also aware (as I discuss in Chapter 2) of the responsibility the participants gave me to make public their perspectives on literacy. When as author I craft their stories, I attempt to draw them fully. I contemplate their experiences by presenting and reflecting on their narratives along with them. I get at one kind of re(presentation) based on the way I knew the four participants, yet in choosing to focus on a certain version of a story (even by choosing a particular coding scheme), I choose also to overlook others that might hold significance. When I write to Melissa more recently about Chief and George and Violeta and Lee Ann, I can barely remember their real names; I am so accustomed to knowing them by pseudonym. I want readers to know these four people and understand their words the way they intended them. I want to be honest in the act of contemplating the participants' narratives over time. But every story is only one person's version of self and events in the moment it is being told by the speaker/writer to the listener/writer. Constructions of self, of material conditions, of oppression and experience, all change. Even the meaning of literacy changes as the four participants perform literate acts in new contexts. And so I continue, along with them, to try to understand literacy as *they* define it.

4

Literacy and Nonliteracy: Reflective Knowledge and Critical Consciousness

IN CHAPTERS 2 AND 3, I EXAMINED MY choice of how to "stand under" the discourses of participants by making my voice the Other, and in this way I have taken on Ratcliffe's project of rhetorical listening. At this point in the book, I choose to return to a more conventional academic format. I flip *standing under* again, back to *understanding,* so that readers and I can do a different kind of work. With the words spoken and written by the four participants in the front of our minds, my hope is that together we can read and understand more analytically than in the previous narrative chapters, yet with the participants' perspectives guiding that analysis.

The participants' comments demonstrate that expressing lived experiences as knowledge depends on having an audience. Their remarks made me aware of how I functioned as a witness by interviewing them and by recording and reflecting on their stories. Even early on, in my first role of classroom observer, my presence offered them a mirror in which to acknowledge that what they related revealed the knowledge of their lived experiences. Being acknowledged, whether by a group of like-minded peers or by a single interested researcher, can provide the validation people need to recognize the value of their own knowledge. And having one's perspective acknowledged makes that knowledge real. Telling or writing what they know helps people to believe that they *do* know, that they are, through their spoken and written words, bearers of knowledge. I tried to make it clear to Lee Ann, George, Violeta, and Chief that my goal in collecting their writing and in speaking with them was to listen and to document what they said, and in this way I hope to have acknowledged their knowledge without appropriating their stories. But seeing adult learners as reflective, critical thinkers depends too on their having their experiences acknowledged by people outside of their peer group at the Read/Write/Now Adult Learning Center and people other than me, a researcher. It depends on readers recognizing the validity of that knowledge.

In this chapter, I examine how the four participants position themselves as nonliterates who have gained literacy. All reflect regularly on their life experiences, and all of them can talk easily about their personal literacy histories. When prompted, they can also talk about the ways they have been oppressed because of their position as nonliterates and about the understanding they have developed throughout their lives about how power operates. They illustrate how literacy is a form of power by describing what it is like to live without literacy. When they speak with me, they are often talking about power relations. In their different ways, Lee Ann, George, Violeta, and Chief critique power relations and reveal how they have learned to confront their social position. Their experience has already provided them with the perspective they need to think critically and to use their critical consciousness to begin to change their lives. Now that they are becoming more literate, they are developing the "tactical knowledge" (Mathieu) and the "tools" (Cushman, *Struggle*) that will enable them to act on what they know.

Throughout the chapter, I explore a form of knowing that involves reflecting on one's experiences to inform present understanding. This reflective knowledge, combined with the participants' critical consciousness, is important to teachers and literacy workers when we think about what matters in literacy education. We can learn by more fully regarding the alternative forms of knowing that people rely on besides school-based knowledge. Yet, when the four participants tell stories from their everyday lives, they are often unaware that their narratives express anything in particular; only when an outsider interprets their words is the wisdom of their daily practices illuminated. As Flower points out, "Historically silenced and marginalized people may not realize their own expertise, may

not have the rhetorical tools to explain and elaborate it, and may ✓
not trust the outcome of personal disclosure or speaking out" (55).
Their distrust occurs because knowledge is socially stratified. Cook-
Gumperz explains that historically, "the knowledge of the *less* literate came to be seen as *lesser knowledge*" (35).

Nonliterate people are usually given credit in the mainstream
only for their practical, commonsense knowledge. Although many
of the tasks they perform throughout their day are ones that re-
quire a great deal of experience and skill (making home repairs,
cooking, negotiating with bosses or landlords), they do not usually
view these activities as knowledge. De Certeau separates ordinary
knowledge into two concepts, *savoir-faire*, "know-how," and *un
faire*, "how-to-do" (69). About *savoir-faire,* he notes, "Know-how
takes on the appearance of an 'intuitive' or 'reflex' ability, which
is almost invisible and whose status remains unrecognized" (69).
The four participants engage with these forms of knowledge daily,
using both *savoir-faire* and *un faire,* but often without recognizing that what they know is knowledge per se. However, they also
have conceptual knowledge of how literacy operates. They know
how they are being gazed upon by bosses and other people who
exert power over them, and they know how to subvert those gazes,
as their spoken and written narratives show. Although they speak
through experience when they tell their stories in this chapter, the
participants are not talking just *about* experience. They speak of
literacy and nonliteracy as experts who are theorizing about what
they know; they *are* literacy critics and researchers. In this vein, I
argue that their spoken and written words about their literacy experiences reveal their knowledge and critical consciousness but in
ways they may not necessarily recognize as anything special. They
don't see themselves as developing a literacy theory, yet they are
perfectly able to do so when prompted to talk about literacy. They
understand literacy in a way that academics do not.

Although the participants are aware of what they do not know in
terms of the lack they connect to nonliteracy, they also talk about
many areas of life about which they are knowledgeable. I coded their
transcripts and writing for occasions when they spoke of knowing

and not knowing. This search revealed that people express various understandings and definitions of what they "know," "don't know," and "want to know." In general, "know" indicated ability (e.g., how to do a math exercise, drive a car or do a job, handle parenting situations appropriately, relate to and have empathy for other people's experiences, carry out workplace responsibilities). People also generalized about things they "don't know." These included inabilities (e.g., "before I don't know how to read my appointment, the bill" [Violeta]), but more often "not knowing" referred to things or situations about which someone was unaware, such as uncertainty about how (and whether) to speak Spanish or English. George spoke of other people not knowing that he was nonliterate, a kind of ignorance he recognized in others that he wanted to control.

I turn now to the four participants to consider what they say and write about how they know literacy, and how, through their narratives and our conversations, they articulate wisdom that comes out of everyday life experience. Their wisdom provides the basis for the critical consciousness they bring to their literacy studies.

LEE ANN: DISCLAIMING WHAT SHE KNOWS

Although she is often emphatic about the limits of her knowledge, Lee Ann is clear about the effects of nonliteracy on her life and the lives of her peers. Her comments suggest that she has suffered all her life from not knowing the discourse of schooling. Lee Ann believes she had an undiagnosed learning disability: "Well, it was hard for me to, you know, like I couldn't tell time. And the, and the teacher got so frustrated with me. . . . And the principal came and sat down with me and tried to get me to tell time. . . . I just couldn't get it, you know? My mind couldn't put it together." Lee Ann is certain that her not knowing was a mix of learning disabilities and emotional difficulties. Even now, she admits, she has to learn slowly and only take in a bit at a time "because that's all my mind could sponge in."

Not knowing what was expected of her in school was exacerbated by her mother's refusal to encourage her literacy practices. In Chapter 2, Lee Ann recalls that her mother denied her any reading materials. She is sure that her obsession with collecting books even when she could not read them is a result of her mother's refusal to treat her like a capable, thinking person. Lee Ann is still infuriated today by her mother's deliberate choice to keep her in a place of ignorance. In the following excerpt, I am reading aloud comments Lee Ann made about her mother in a previous interview, and she is responding:

> LEE ANN: She probably didn't want to encourage it when I was a kid to read. Didn't care if I knew how to read. It's sad.
>
> LAUREN: Why is that?
>
> LA: 'Cause an, 'cause an education person can find out things about their self that, that, that down life's road. Right? . . . My life is a mystery, but I don't want to go into it because, you know something, I don't want to open a can of worms. You know?

Lee Ann speculates about the ability that she believes literate people have in contrast to her own experience, which has given her less opportunity to reflect or analyze. Occasionally she's wistful about how her life "is a mystery" that she hasn't been able to fully figure out. Whether that mystery is the result of personal trauma or a learning disability or other factors, Lee Ann connects education with an understanding of self. She assumes there are kinds of self-knowledge that other people have, and she is able to articulate what it is she imagines they know.

Lee Ann practically insists that she does not have the wisdom gained through experience, that her difficulty learning has left her unable to examine her own experiences. But as we probe her transcripts and texts, she is perfectly able to analyze her own life. She has a great deal of reflective knowledge about literacy and nonliteracy, yet she discredits herself. Lee Ann is very much aware of the power of literacy and how it has been used against her, as she made clear in her story about getting kicked out of the church choir. She is quick to relate incidents of being "kicked to the curb," whether by employers, choir directors, or her own mother. Lee Ann recalls the way she used to record her mother's violations of her:

> I don't meditate on what happened to me when I was a child. But it's funny. When I started writing letters with it, thinking back when I was a child, the, the marks on the wall came back to me. 'Cause I forgot about it for fifty years, never thought about it for fifty years. And I remember, you know, hey, I used to get—. She used to punish me, and I used to put a mark against her, and that's how I released my thing. I didn't go crazy—breaking, running through our house, break anything like kids do today, or kids kill their parents or anything—I just marked it and . . . Another count against you being mean to me, another count, you know, another mark on the wall. Then every time I got five, because I couldn't count, but I just crossed it.

Learning to write at Read/Write/Now not only provides Lee Ann the opportunity to reflect differently on her past, but she says that it also helps her to recall events she claims to have forgotten ("When I started writing letters with it . . . the marks on the wall came back to me."). Still, when she describes her system of recording groups of five marks on the wall, Lee Ann claims she is unable to count. She demonstrates how she kept a record while simultaneously insisting that she lacked the ability to do so. It is difficult to know to what extent Lee Ann truly sees herself as unable to accumulate knowledge through her life experiences, or whether she has been so convinced of her own unworthiness that she continually invalidates her understanding.

She doesn't have a lot of writing in her portfolio. Lee Ann isn't ready yet. She is still putting together sentences word by word and doubting herself in the process. One of the few pieces she did complete during her year at Read/Write/Now was this narrative about the situation in her family:

No More Pretending
Lee Ann

Growing up I had to pretend that things were ok. The man who raised me was an alcoholic. He used to tell me I wasn't his kid. It made me feel sad. My mother used to hit me with a belt. I would go into the bathroom and put marks on the wall for every time she hit me. The wall was covered with marks because she hit me so much. My mother dominated me my whole life. That made me be a people pleaser. I wanted people to like me. So I put on a mask. I would pretend that things were fine. I would be happy on the outside but crying on the inside.

My mother never had a picture of me. It was like she did not want me to exist. I never turned my back on her though. I took care of her until she died. Growing up I had to pretend that things were fine. I kept to myself and never let anyone know that I was having problems at home. All my life she put me down. Now I do not wear a mask anymore. I let people know how I feel. I don't hide my feelings anymore. If I am upset at someone, I tell them how I'm feeling. It's good not to pretend.

When Lee Ann talks about her experiences, she undercuts herself, or she starts to spin out from an observation or analytical statement into a rant about something like herbal cures for cancer or the Bible. But her essay "No More Pretending," unlike her remarks, shows narrative control, perhaps because she revised it a few times with a teacher's support. Overall, though, Lee Ann tends to attribute other people, institutions, or even books as more valid sources of knowledge than her own experience. She imagines that if she raids texts and unlocks what is inside them she will have the answers—the cures—to her troubles.

Just as her own life story remains mysterious to Lee Ann, the knowledge contained within books seems to retain mysterious power. She wants that knowledge, yet she is still unconvinced that she can "sponge [it] in." There are, however, some forms of knowledge she will claim, such as the ability to make complicated financial arrangements (although she asks for help reading and paying her bills) and driving. Lee Ann speaks so often about driving and expresses her pride in giving people rides that I began to understand how driving functions as a metaphor for a certain kind of knowledge that she is sure she possesses. She explains, "When I got a driver's license, the world was open to me more because I could get around, didn't have to beg anybody to take me to the store; I was independent." Driving, for Lee Ann, is a form of literacy. The driver's license is the standard for how things change when one becomes more literate: "I got a driver's license. Because, I tell you, that was all a *miracle* for me. Anybody would take that for granted, but for me, in my life, because I can't read, that was the miracle. I tell you, that was a miracle."

Boasting about her driving prowess is one of the few occasions when Lee Ann claims any confidence about the knowledge she possesses. However, although her tendency is to disclaim her own knowledge, she is assertive in expressing her opinions regarding herbs and natural healing, what she might tell the president if she were to write him a letter, and how she understands the Bible. These emphatic statements of belief sometimes constitute reflective knowledge; for example, Lee Ann's remarks about her driver's license being a miracle for a nonliterate person suggest that she has been thinking about the relationship between driving and reading for a long time. She also sometimes voices critical consciousness, as when she criticizes the president's position on war. Although some of her views oppose dominant perspectives, Lee Ann is inconsistent about trusting herself.

Aside from driving, one of the few other forms of reflective knowledge that Lee Ann claims with conviction is insight into her shared experience—a collective awareness with her peers at Read/Write/Now—as a nonliterate person. Here Lee Ann reflects on the reading of a program-wide publication, focusing on a piece by a woman named Theresa whose narrative reminds Lee Ann of herself:

> LEE ANN: Teacher had everybody read their own story, and I, and I said, I relate to [a] lot of them. And then I relate to, uh, they almost had identical, same stories, like Theresa did. But had to move from place to place. . . . Her, too, her family moved place to place. How can you get settled in a school when you move three times a year? How can you really, you know, get to know the other classmates

and, and get a ball rolling when, you know. . . ?

LAUREN: What can somebody else get from reading your story?

LA: Well, probably went through the same thing. Maybe they had an alcoholic father, too. . . . Well, I, I relate to them. Just like an alcoholic relates to an alcoholic and you all go, and it's the reason why for everything when he go, like I said, go to AA or something like that, everybody tells a story to help each other out in AA meetings. They go to AA meetings to, to get inspired by the higher power and stop their alcohol, stop their drugs, because all of them programs are, are really wonderful. A lot of them do really stop and get help.

In this passage, when Lee Ann poses a series of questions about being constantly unsettled and therefore unable to absorb school literacy, her answers are clearly implied: You cannot get settled in a school when you move three times a year. You cannot consistently learn. You cannot accumulate literacy when school instruction is always interrupted and your life is unstable. In posing these questions, Lee Ann expresses the wisdom of her lived experience. Lee Ann isn't the only one to have suffered; other people like Theresa have suffered also in parallel situations. The experience of growing up without sufficient literacy and grappling with its effects throughout her life has provided Lee Ann with wisdom. This reflective knowledge of her shared experience gives her insights into others.

Lee Ann takes her point further when she compares the work that gets accomplished in the center with an Alcoholics Anonymous meeting. She implies that in both settings people have the appropriate insights to offer one another, that their self-knowledge can be important to their peers' learning process, and that in relating to her peers she also learns to understand herself better. In AA and at Read/Write/Now, people get to know one another by developing a collective understanding of their struggles, which they then can apply to their own personal growth and to the knowledge of the group. When Lee Ann makes a comparison between AA and learning at Read/Write/Now, she is demonstrating her reflective knowledge and critical awareness as someone who can comment on the ways knowledge is used in similar contexts.

GEORGE: ACCUMULATING EXPERIENTIAL WISDOM

In contrast to Lee Ann, the other three participants are confident in identifying and sometimes even theorizing about areas of their lives in which they are knowledgeable. Like Lee Ann, George talks about the *savoir-faire* and *un faire* (de Certeau) he relied on when he was nonliterate, discussing the knowledge that bosses and co-workers had of him and how he was able to control the way they gazed on him through his workplace performance. George created a knowledgeable workplace self based on the confidence that he could teach himself anything. Although he remembers school as "terrible" and essentially worthless, he speaks eloquently about the informal learning he acquired as a boy growing up on a farm in the South, which was about how to work hard. His bravado about himself as a worker is a display of his everyday knowing, the interplay of *savoir-faire* and *un faire*. He knows how to do it; his experiential knowledge has given him the confidence to enter new situations and accumulate knowledge.

Because George could rely on his keen sense of observation, he was able to teach himself the skills he needed at work even when he was unable to read and write. He could cover for himself with his tactical knowledge (see de Certeau; Mathieu) and without compromising his presentation of himself as a capable worker. Still, George was acutely aware of the skills he was missing: "I never been in school, I didn't know nothing, but it didn't really bother me." The alternative learning he developed had to be thorough and precise if he was going to pass. He created a process of close observation and memorization that involved continual reflection on how and why a task had to be done a certain way. George's methods gave him greater access to learning than a literate person might gain by reading a manual. Each step in his process of observing, memorizing, and reflecting required that he measure what he was learning against what he had already experienced and integrate new knowledge with past experiences. Everything had to be stored in his head.

George's boastful references to being the second highest paid man in the shop and to having that information posted show how important it is to his self-worth to have his achievements acknowledged publicly. This display of workplace prowess gave him a sense of his value as a worker and earner and, therefore, as a person. But complicating George's pride was his preoccupation with how people interpreted him. He craved recognition as a way to keep people from knowing that he was nonliterate. He wanted to maintain a view of himself that he could control. Still, despite the complex acts of self-teaching, performing, and sustaining a certain persona, George admits that his lack of education was always "in the back of my mind."

Because his knowledge was experiential and observational, it was specific to the context of his job at the forge. George had to face his "not knowing" when the shop closed, and he had to take stock of himself as he prepared to pursue new employment. How much weight did the knowledge he had developed at the forge carry into other contexts? And how might that knowledge transfer into future employment possibilities and into his worth as an individual? This change of life events forced George to assess himself, and he was reminded of two things: that he was getting older (implying that his value as a physical laborer may have lessened) and that he might want something other than a "hard job" that involves constant and intense heat, heavy metal, and unflinching focus. But the process of reflection, as George recalls, also involved thinking back over his assets and being reminded of his vulnerability—that he had no formal education, that in the view of potential employers—and perhaps in his own view of himself—he "didn't know nothing."

George and I talk about how writing enables him to tell other people what he knows. We examine the early draft of a piece he composed called "Be Careful What You Wish For" in which he writes about his first credit card experience and how

> I lean how to use the card the right way instead of useing the card so must now I just use money but a credit card is are good thing to have because sometime that is all you need I have learn my lesson now.

I ask George what it might be important to communicate to other people in this cautionary narrative about the danger of running up a credit card bill.

Be careful, you know. Because, you see, if you never experienced something, if you never did it before, then this is like a . . . a car. A new car. You never had a car before. You, first you get a car, you don't have no experience with that car, never *had* a car before, so you, you going to take some unnecessarily challenges and do some things that you don't suppose [you're not supposed to] but, and once something *happen*, then you begin to realize that, that you should have been more cautious, you should have. You know all kind of things run through your mind then. Then you begin to learn that, what having a car, what it take to take care of it and different things like that, so that would be like the same thing that you speaking about a credit card. You know what I mean?

The inexperienced driver, just like the first-time credit card owner, makes mistakes and may get into trouble. George crafts the examples of car ownership and credit card use into an explicit lesson that shows how the driver and the credit card owner learn to be more cautious by reflecting on their own actions. At age sixty-one, George sees himself as the bearer of experiential, reflective knowledge that he can pass on to others. If a person reads George's "Be Careful" narrative, will he get something out of it? "I think so. . . . I really do. I think so. Because you know if you, if somebody would read it, well, he or she could say, well, that a person, that person that did that experience, that he probably know what he's talking about, you know?"

From his position as someone who "knows" based on a lifetime of experience in the workplace and in social settings, George also expresses the critical consciousness that some theorists argue people must be taught (Giroux, *Border Crossings,* "Literacy" ; McLaren; Shor). Chapter 1 opens with an example of George telling a story about a time when he was standing in line at the supermarket and realized that a woman ahead of him could not read signs at the register. Here is that scene again:

I think it was the store somewhere, and um, the person was ahead of me. She didn't know what she was doing because— see this big sign right there? But it's just like I say: You don't know how to read and write . . . you don't know what that sign up there saying. And I was able to assist [her], to show her. I didn't do it in a way to make myself look big, doing the way to try to embarrass her 'cause of other peoples behind me. . . . I put it in a way, like, "Well, you just didn't see that, didn't see that word." But I know she saw that word; she didn't know what it is. You don't do it [help someone read] to try to harm someone else, make yourself look big, . . . you do something to try to help somebody . . . in a way that you won't embarrass the person; you know what I mean? . . . 'Cause you got to look at the time when, when you couldn't read or write. I look at it myself . . . somebody had embarrassed me too. Oh yeah, I been embarrassed. It got to the point: "Well, can't you read?" And do you know? I can't. [*laughs*] . . . "You can't read!"

In the following discussion of that scene, George unknowingly echoes Freire (*Pedagogy*) and Elspeth Stuckey, who both theorize how literacy becomes social "violence" when it is wielded as a weapon to denigrate and oppresses some citizens.

    GEORGE: Let's say a group of people sitting around. He or she know some of these people can't read or write. Now, why give a person, let's say a sheet of paper like this with all these word on it? Now, you know good and well he or she could not read this paper, and you know it in your heart that they couldn't. Why would you do that [ask them to read the paper]? You know, to embarrass these people around the other people? Now, I'm not talking about in class [at Read/Write/Now], I'm just talking about, you know?

    LAUREN: Right.

    G: Right. And while this may embarrass you, and you know they couldn't, you know, couldn't read. I could see somebody do that that didn't know, what do you say, uh, "Well, I didn't know he or she couldn't read. Or, I wouldn't have never given, you know, given them word." But somebody do it *intentionally*, knowing that person can't read, I think that's a *shameful* thing to do to a person; you know what I mean?

L: I think, I think I know what you mean. I think you mean if somebody intentionally—

G: *Yeah! Intentionally!*

L: —gives you something that you can't read, it's like, it's like they're sort of pulling a power move on you. Like—

G: Yeah! . . .

L: And you think people do that?

G: Oh, yeah. People do it. People do it. People do it when— I would never do that to nobody. I wouldn't do it because . . . everybody (just like I said before), everybody wasn't able to get a education. And because you got it, that don't mean you supposed to put somebody else down because you have it; you know what I mean? If anything, you do anything; you try to do something to help somebody else. You know, help somebody else. Pull them up, not try to, you know, push them down. You know?

George's words show his critical consciousness: a literate person who is aware of another person's nonliteracy can choose to treat the nonliterate person with respect by helping her, or he can use his position to embarrass and subjugate. The person who has had the benefit of education is always in control. The way George sees it, it is the responsibility of the literate individual to know and think critically about power relations for the purpose of changing things. George demonstrates how he, as someone who is now crossing a border between nonliteracy and literacy (Giroux, *Border Crossings*), has taken on a new kind of knowledge. He has the benefit of the new literacies he has acquired; he also has the reflective and analytical knowledge he has gained throughout his lifetime. Together, his reflective knowledge and his critical consciousness enable him to interact differently in the world. His perspective is shifting, providing him with increasing awareness. Because George now knows something he didn't used to know, he has also taken on the responsibility of using that knowledge wisely. His words imply that becoming literate entails a certain responsibility, that the literate person should know how to use his knowledge to help others rather than to insult them. But this knowledge is also specific to someone like George, who has acquired literacy later in life and who already has a wealth of understanding about how power operates. He is able to use his critical consciousness to explain that literate people can choose to interrupt the cycle of denigrating nonliterate people. His idea that this cycle can be disrupted is reminiscent of Fanon's belief (originating in Hegel) that the colonized and the colonizer can break the circle that locks them into the positions of "settler" (*Wretched*) and "other" (*Black Skin* 217–18) (see Chapter 6).

In our dialogue, George demonstrates his ability to theorize about literacy. His discussion of what he knows does more than display critical rhetoric; George is challenging prescribed ideas about education by critically examining the behaviors of those who denigrate nonliterate people. He does this to articulate his principles about how nonliteracy operates. The literate oppressor "*intentionally*" will "push them down" as a way to subjugate and maintain control. By explaining how the pattern operates, George demonstrates that he has worked through these ideas over time, based on a set of consistent guiding principles that he developed from his own experiences. To this extent, he theorizes about literacy as social violence on his own terms. His experience has allowed him to develop and apply an elaborate system of critique.

VIOLETA: PRAGMATIC KNOWLEDGE, REFLECTIVE KNOWLEDGE, AND RESTORYING

Whereas George looks back over the expanse of his life and recasts his experiences as lessons narrated by a wise elder, Violeta expresses a desire to "progress" based on her personal process of evaluating her experiences, pursuing new forms of knowledge, and taking action based on what she discovers. Being more literate is part of a process of moving away from a position in which other people have had power over her toward an independent self who has more control over her life.

Violeta does not, however, follow a traditional trajectory of progress. A dominant path toward literacy dictates that adult learners work to obtain a GED and workplace skills so they can become more functional members of society. Violeta does hope to get her GED someday and become a social worker, but she is not motivated primarily by dominant expectations. The circumstances of her daily life as a single mother of six and a grandmother, a welfare recipient, a Spanish speaker who still struggles to use English, an older learner, and an HIV patient already prevent Violeta from pursuing a mainstream route toward education. Her ability even to stay in the program at Read/Write/Now depends on her child care responsibilities, which shift as children change schools or bring their own babies home to live under her care. When Violeta talks about progress, she refers to her long-term intention of changing her life.

Literacy is a way for Violeta to learn to "depend about myself" (see Chapter 2). This means not having to ask other people to make appointments and phone calls on her behalf. It means reading her own mail and understanding official papers she is asked to sign. The independence she seeks is itself a form of knowledge that allows her to participate in society more effectively as a self-possessed and knowing citizen. Violeta speaks frequently about the sense of fear that used to dominate her social interactions and how education is helping her to confront that oppression. Now she can use reading and writing "[to] get out [in] front of the world."

√ There is a lot more to seeking literacy than attaining functional skills. Violeta's lived experience has taught her to interact with the world in certain ways, and she already knows how to successfully "make do" (de Certeau) and care for her children and grandchildren. But at the same time, she speaks about a different kind of knowledge—an exploration into herself—that she is able to achieve through writing: "I like to write; . . . my teacher right now teaching me how to write a letter for another person. Yeah, I want to know what did I put it over there? I want my writing to read it back. I

want to learn, see I write some letter for somebody, the person understand what did I write in the paper."

Violeta is expressing two kinds of knowledge simultaneously: pragmatic knowledge and reflective knowledge. Her awareness of how to function in society (the pragmatic *savoir-faire* and *un faire*) and her desire for the self-improvement she gains by carving out time for herself so that she can develop other forms of knowledge (reflective knowledge) overlap. Reading and writing are activities she engages in for herself when her children are at school, and Read/Write/Now provides her with a space of her own where she can study apart from her family. Literacy allows her to create a different relationship with herself. In her previous comment, Violeta contrasts her more introspective goals for writing with her practical purposes for reading, such as understanding bills and appointments. "Read it back" implies that both she and an audience outside herself can read her writing and benefit by reflecting on it. The person she connects with in a letter can understand her words and think about them. Violeta's description of a shifting relationship with herself as she continues her education suggests that a kind of textual agency emerges through the act of engaging with texts, particularly with her own writing.

Violeta finds too that writing offers her an opportunity to re-story her experiences and that in the act of retelling she is creating a new form of self-knowledge. The process of restorying (Connelly and Clandinin; Freeman; Mahala and Swilky) is about the choice to tell a story another way, as Violeta explains when she reflects on her decision to write about a certain aspect of her life: "Let me start it again. Let me start it again, writing now." Telling her life story through writing permits her to self-analyze by relying on the new perspective she is gaining when she composes herself on the page. Each time she reads through her portfolio, her "life book," she examines the stories against one another, continually revising her experience, and in the process she creates a new narrative. This is how Violeta challenges her autobiographical scripts.

For example, Violeta wrote "Taking Off the Masks" for the publication *The Masks We Wear*.[1] Writing about masks was part of a program-wide project on mask making.[2] In this poem, she is critical of situations in her life and actively alters her subject position.

Taking Off the Masks
Violeta Blanca

When I couldn't speak English, it was a mask
No more masks
No more translator

When I was with my husband, it was a mask
No more masks
No more husband

When I was pregnant with Jared, it was a mask
No more masks
No more miscarriage

When I think about my nephews, it was a mask
No more masks
No more visitors

When I lived with my stepfather, it was a mask
No more masks
No more running away

When I argued with my daughter about school, it was a mask
No more masks
No more arguments

Then she composed another piece, "My Mask," which she submitted anonymously. "My Mask" is the first published text in which Violeta does not adopt a recommended structure; instead, she tells her story as a prose narrative.

My Mask

I wear my mask everyday. I use my mask with my children, in this class, and with my mother and my friend. My mask hides my sadness. When I take my medicine with my son, I pretend it is a game. I do not want my son to be worried. When I read, my mask goes away because reading makes me feel much better. When I wake up in the morning I see my children and I say to God, "thank you." I wear my mask to hide my HIV. Everyday I have to fight with HIV. Sometimes I get tired, but when I see my children, I know I have to live with HIV. My son does not know he lives with HIV, so again, I put on a mask. I know one day I'm going to win my fight with HIV. Then I can take off my mask for good.

In "Taking Off the Masks," Violeta used the refrain "it was a mask" to mean "it was a bad situation." But "My Mask" uses the metaphor of masking to reveal a hidden story; and in writing it, Violeta gives herself the chance to take off her mask. She is not simply playing with images or spelling out the conditions of her life. Instead Violeta uses the metaphor of masking to analyze a complicated situation. She does this work to "tell," "retell," and "relive" her experiences (Connelly and Clandinin), and in this way she revises her prior understanding of herself.

By choosing to publish this narrative, Violeta decided to unmask herself in writing, though the content of the piece explains that she is rarely unmasked in her daily life. Her presentation of a shifting self illustrates James Britton's theory of the increasingly experienced writer who becomes able to participate in events again as a "spectator" of her own life. When Violeta writes in spectator mode, she is reinterpreting a common discourse of the individual who is improved by literacy. She wants to retell her story, and she wants to interact in the world with greater *autho*rity and independence. She has the knowledge to transform herself.

CHIEF: THE PLEASURE OF LITERACY

Of all the participants, Chief is most secure in his identity as someone who "knows" from the wisdom of his collected experiences. He expresses enthusiasm about all of his new literacies, and he wants to share his discoveries with others. Chief is generous about his impulse not only to share his wisdom but also to interest people in his interests and to encourage others to make the choices he has made.

In addition to being a learner at Read/Write/Now, Chief is involved in other communities. He is a trustee at his church and president of the church choir, and he sings in a couple of men's gospel groups. He talks about the songwriting he does with one group:

> CHIEF: . . . I sing with another group. . . . And we are cutting a CD. I'm writing the songs for this group. We're, we write our own songs. We're getting ready to do a recording. I hope we get it out.
>
> LAUREN: . . . So, when you sing in the church group and with these guys, do you need to know how to read the music? Write? Or the lyrics?
>
> C: We, we write our songs so we learn them as we write them. And that way we don't have, we don't have no books to read from either. You, uh, you ever see the quartet groups?
>
> L: Mm hmm.
>
> C: They write their own stuff then learn it as you write it.
>
> L: Right. But somebody's got to be writing it down, to remember.
>
> C: No, we remember, we remember; you memorize it.
>
> L: And that's it?
>
> C: I got two, three songs. This one right here [*we're looking at a photograph of the members of the quartet*], he could write

a song. . . . He could write a song, this one. He could
write a song. I never seen anyone, uh, the guy could write
a song, put a song together so quick.

The song "writing" Chief refers to is an oral process; there is no
written documentation. Composing and learning happen through
memorization. Since I assume that Chief has been composing lyrics longer than he has been literally writing, it becomes clear that
"writing" creatively was already something Chief did before he attended Read/Write/Now.

When I insist that someone in the group must be recording the
lyrics and music, I reveal my ignorance. Musicians in the gospel
quartet practice a different kind of literacy when they compose,
memorize, and eventually record a CD. My misconception that
they must be writing as a way to remember exposes one of my
weaknesses as an academic researcher who privileges writing over
other means of making knowledge permanent. When Chief cor-
rects me, I am also made aware of his choice of the word *write*
to mean "create" lyrics and music. The composing process Chief
refers to is one of creating without writing. A person can be literate
or nonliterate and still be a songwriter in the quartet.[3] He and the
other quartet members have been "writing" successfully for years
without the technology of writing. There is no need to write to
know. While Chief's description of the group does not preclude
writing or his practicing other literacies, he never implies that his
music would be better or worse if the group were literally to write
down their words and music.

Unlike the majority of learners I have met at Read/Write/Now,
Chief confidently expresses awareness of what he knows and how
well he knows himself. He is not at Read/Write/Now for personal
discovery in the way that Violeta is. Chief is there because he wants
to have an opportunity denied him earlier in his life. As a retired
person, he has the time and interest in developing new literacies
simply because he wants to. In the following segment, he and I
are examining a comment he made in a previous interview when
he talked about reading and writing as something he had always
wanted to do and as a way to "better" himself.

L: Do you think that a person is better if he knows more about reading and writing?

C: No, what I mean about better myself, means a better—better to read. Not because I, I never want to change. I want to be myself. But when I say, when I speak of bettering myself it means, better—learn better how to read. And, uh, speech. And, uh, using proper words. That's what I mean by better myself. But physically, I'm going to stay me.

L: Not becoming a better, morally better person?

C: No, no. I think, I want to be, I don't ever want to get changed by the way I am because I want to be nice to everybody, and that's the way I want to, I want to treat everybody nice. That's the way I want to be all my life. . . . I want to be just like I raised up to be.

L: Mm hmm, and that has nothing to do with reading and writing?

C: Nothing to do with reading and writing.

L: So it's a different kind of bettering yourself?

C: Yes. It's better—the only thing I'm saying, when I speak of better myself—better in education.

Chief is emphatic about knowing who he is and being satisfied with himself already. Knowing himself does not have to do with reading and writing.

One of Chief's distinguishing features is his warm humor. He wants to have a good time, and he sees literacy study as a pursuit of pleasure, as he explains: "And that's the way I like to, that's the way I enjoy life, 'cause you were not put here—I had enough bad luck when I was coming up so I want to be happy now. . . . And I want everybody else to be happy." Being happy for Chief includes pursuing new literacies. His comments about the pleasure he finds in learning illuminate how becoming more literate because it is pleasurable can have little to do with accruing cultural capital to become a "better" person. He talks about this when we review the transcript in which he described how reading "opened up a new world for me":

I been reading about ancient history and all that. And it's stuff that I like to know about. I didn't know all these things. And I read about books about, ah, ancient history all back in, uh, Christopher Columbus and all that. . . . And I read that book and I get—I love—I love to read about the ancient history. I love reading about, ah, African American, ah, American Indians. I read quite a few books.

Chief's exclamation that he reads because he loves it begs the question of how dominant discourses of literacy deal with pleasure. Is pleasure valued in our culture as a primary motivation for learning? Chief's delight in becoming more literate is reflected in his engagement with every aspect of his education. In one of our conversations, he reflects on the overwhelming joy he felt when he first read aloud to his peers at the center and realized that he was capable of writing and sharing his own words publicly:

> C: I was, I, when I wrote, first piece that I wrote, I don't
> know if it was because I was so proud of it, and, uh,
> you know, like at the end of the year we would read out
> what had, what we had done. I couldn't read it, I was so
> bubbled up and proud; I was so upset that water was just
> running out of my eyes.
> L: [*laughing*] Because you could do it!
> C: And I could, and I said, I was said: If I had to do this—
> and I made a speech in front of the whole class—I said:
> "Two years ago somebody told me I was doing, I would
> be doing this, I would tell them, no, they was lying. I
> couldn't do it." But hey, I got so bubbled up, I couldn't
> even, I couldn't even do the, couldn't even read the, one
> of the stu—one of the other students had to help me out.
> . . . I had a good feeling I had in me.
> L: Because you could do it?
> C: Yeah. That I had done something like that, and I knowed
> it. And it wasn't that I hadn't been going to school that
> long either.

Chief's pleasure could be seen as simply reflecting the fulfillment he gains from literacy, but his remark that he doesn't want to change—he wants to be the person he already is, but he also wants to read and write better—challenges a dominant discourse dictating that people should want to improve their literacy to improve their self-worth. Chief doesn't want to improve his self (Foucault, "Ethic"). He wants to read so that he can know more. He wants to read so that he can read more. He wants to send out newsletters to fellow learners at Read/Write/Now so that they will want to read more. And he wants to write because he can entertain himself and others.

As I've suggested, writing is not usually linked to pleasure in our national discourse, and few initiatives promote writing in ways similar to reading (see Chapter 6). For Chief, though, writing offers as much pleasure as reading:

> C: I write pretty good, but my spelling; I am working on all of this stuff now, my writing and my spelling.
>
> L: But what you really wanted was the reading? The writing, it sounds like the writing wasn't something that you thought about as much as the reading?
>
> C: Oh yes, the writing—
>
> L: Both of them together?
>
> C: Oh yes, both of—all of that goes together. . . . When I'll say reading, that means writing, the whole works. I need to learn math, all of that: write, math, spelling. I've come a long ways, since I've been here, and I'm very proud of myself for what I've accomplished. I always loved to read, wanted to read the Bible. Now I read the Bible every night. And, uh, I also love to read now. I read books. When I am usually at home, I'm reading if I am not doing something around the house.

When I asked Chief to select the writing in his portfolio that made him proudest, he pointed to his funny stories: "I like little jokes about, sometimes about, . . . uh, let's see. . . . Little something. I like [to] do things to make me laugh or enjoy." I was curious why he liked his humorous writing best when I found some of his more serious narratives more compelling. But he helped me realize that sharing his pleasure with others is important. "Chief and Rabbit" is the narrative Chief claimed to like best because it was about something that really happened and because it is meant to make readers laugh at the narrator who, once confounded, was eventually able to outsmart a rabbit in his garden.

Chief and Rabbit

I must say, the first two weeks of my vacation this little rabbit almost drove me crazy. Every time I turned around that rabbit was in my vegetable garden. I'd run him out and go into the house. I'd look back out in the garden and there he would be again. I thought about taking a rock and killing him and making rabbit stew out of him. But my wife wouldn't let me so we had to come to up with something else. So I watched the rabbit to see where the rabbit went when my wife chased him. I watched him to see where he went through the fence. Then I got a sack and put it where he ran through the fence. When my wife chased him, I was ready. I put the sack down by the fence. My wife chased him. I lay down so when my wife chased him again, he ran into the sack. I pulled the sack up and said, "I've got him." My wife said, "You and your rabbit!"

Chief has crafted a story, something he does with increasing comfort. The narrator of "Chief and Rabbit" is not so much befuddled as he is challenged to solve a problem. By adopting a folktale style, Chief demonstrates how he uses his wits to rid himself of the rabbit while at the same time humoring his wife. Chief the narrator is resourceful and successful in his strategy, and he is a good storyteller. Chief says he liked this particular narrative because the situation amused him. But Royster reminds us that "simple" storytelling, which has always been valued in the African American community, simultaneously does the work of "theorizing in narrative form" (35). Chief's apparently "simple" stories, and his terse notes from the editor, can "be perceived not just as 'simple stories' to delight and entertain but as vital layers of a transformative process" (35). He doesn't explicitly position himself as a literacy theorist, of course, but Chief often theorizes about what he knows and what he believes others can know based on his example; in this case, he demonstrates the resourcefulness of his problem-solving character and the narrative control of his storyteller.

In *A Rhetoric of Pleasure*, T. R. Johnson identifies five kinds of pleasure that he observes in college students' writing (the solo pleasure of the composing process itself, sharing one's writing with another person who may also enjoy listening to and interacting with the writer, having a muse or other person outside oneself onto whom pleasure is projected, believing in a certain "magic" of writing [Elbow, "Writing and Magic"], and experiencing pleasure as the opposite of pain), but only a few categories apply to the adult learners in this study. For most of them, writing, even when they enjoy it, remains a struggle that reminds them of the most difficult aspects of confronting nonliteracy. Some learners, like Lee Ann, more often experience writing as painful than as a release from pain because it reinforces all they struggle with and feel that they do not know. Chief's writing and interview comments, however, support Johnson's idea that people experience pleasure in the solo act of composing, in the social act of sharing with a reader or listener, and as an act that is joyful.

Chief has taught me about three more types of pleasure, which he expresses in his writing and in his overall relationship to literacy: the pleasure of knowing, the pleasure in learning to write, and literacy as play. Literacy and pleasure are significantly connected for Chief, and he is extremely motivated to keep pursuing literacy. Overall, the enjoyment he speaks of in connection with his studies shows that Chief gains pleasure from viewing himself as knowledgeable. Before he became more literate, Chief already defined himself as a wise elder; now his sense of his own knowledge has broadened, and this awareness makes Chief happy.

AGE AND WISDOM

Ruth Ray and W. Ross Winterowd have both written on the intersections of rhetoric and age studies, asserting that older people write to chronicle and preserve their experiences. Their studies examine older age as a period when people are open to reflecting and speaking out with the confidence that their lives, rich in significant experiential knowledge, have provided them. Ray's focus on gaining wisdom as a process that involves assimilating new stories into older established ones, and looking at narratives in relation to one another, offers an explanation that is useful for investigating the wisdom expressed by the four Read/Write/Now participants. Through my process of meeting with them over multiple interviews and informally to discuss their transcripts and written texts, I was able to revisit their narratives along with them, drawing out different versions of their stories and turning them back to examine certain aspects of their own writing and thinking.

The people in Ray's senior writing groups sought out the Life Story circle as a forum for telling the stories of their lives while they still could while often avoiding painful or negative subjects. But the participant authors in my study, younger than most of Ray's seniors though still close enough in age to have responded to writing in similar ways, do not follow the patterns she observed. Lee Ann, George, Violeta, and Chief tend not to self-censor, avoid, or look toward positive representations of their experiences. More often they exhibit urgency in telling their stories (both orally and in writing), and they don't tidy up the narratives. Their priority is to account for their lives by telling different versions of their stories. Articulating an accurate representation of self is most valuable for these people who previously have not had the privilege of self-representation through writing.

For example, George's remarks tell us that he believes older people carry the wisdom of their lived experiences and that they should be acknowledged as experts. His expansive storytelling style suggests that he places himself in this category of knowing elder. He loves to be asked his view of things, and he seems to find pleasure in opportunities to reflect aloud. George's particular style of oral and written reflection contains some common storytelling features. He uses his own experience to craft cautionary tales that teach a life lesson; we saw this in the narrative about the credit card. Sometimes he adopts a preaching tone, as he does in this piece about his

fiftieth birthday. He used to be a sinner, but he is getting better all
the time.

> One significant birthday when I reached 50 I was so happy
> because I thought that I wood never reach 50. My life style
> was not always good. I use to love to party and party but now
> no more party and no more ranging around. I stop doing all
> of that. Now I just stay at home and in joy my family and go
> to church every Sunday. I am happy now and so gloa [glad]
> that I change my life. No more drink andno more partying.
> Now IM so thank forth to god that part of my life is no more.

George described this piece as "meaningful to me." This was because, he said, he hadn't been sure he would live to fifty; some of
his friends had died already. The narrative holds meaning for him
because he believes other people might look at it as a "confidence
builder." Typically he talks and writes about knowing how to carry
on. As Ray observed about the men in her writing groups, "Older
men tend to focus their life stories around the theme of overcoming
difficulties in the physical world" (62).

Expressing their stories on their terms is vital for George and
his peers partly because outside readers and listeners become witnesses to their experience. It also shows them the impact their own
story might have on others; they already know how great an effect
it has had on them. Retelling their pivotal stories to an interested
outsider provides them with a new opportunity to reflect on what
they know and to shape that story as reflective knowledge. Their
reflective knowledge sometimes combines with critical consciousness, as we see when George explains how literate people sometimes
deliberately shame nonliterates. In that extract, he demonstrates his
understanding of how power operates, thus revealing his critical
consciousness. Referring back to the story of the woman he assisted
in the supermarket, he analyzes the politics of literacy, theorizing
about injustice and oppression. Who knows whether George would
have told this story in this way at an earlier time in his life? Whether
or not his narrative can be linked explicitly to age is irrelevant; what
matters is that he reflects on his experience from the narrative dis-

tance Ray describes, which allows him to contextualize his memories in a particular way and to use his story to make an important point about social injustice.

When Lee Ann spoke about how she relates to her peers at Read/Write/Now, she was suggesting that the community of adult learners offers her validation. Relating to other members of her class helps Lee Ann feel that she is not isolated in her experience. She has witnesses to her story, and some of those witnesses share collective knowledge. By acknowledging that a classmate, Theresa, underwent struggles similar to her own, Lee Ann becomes able to claim what she knows. Although I do not see her theorizing about literacy with the conviction that I find in the other three, I still see Lee Ann moving toward increased personal and social awareness as she critiques material conditions.

Knowledge for Violeta depends on retelling her stories as a way to figure out her life. Her awareness that she is creating new forms of reflective knowledge as she transitions toward a more independent self illustrates how literacy offers the potential for self-transformation. Violeta transitions from viewing herself as someone who is trying hard to take control of her life by adding education to it, to understanding herself as a deeply reflective person who can make sense of experiences in new ways.

A person's awareness of knowing and not knowing can be rife with contradictions, as all four participants demonstrate. Chief recalls the tensions he has faced between what he knows versus what he doesn't know, awareness versus skills, experience versus lack of formal education, and how those oppositions are entwined:

> I was on a job that I could have had got a better position had I known how to read. I didn't know how to read, so it's a lot of hard feelings goes in it too. You know, you feel bad because you don't know these things, you don't know how to read. I've turned down jobs because I knew I couldn't do them because I couldn't read. I always wanted to learn how to read, and now I feel better. I am trying to see if I can get some kind of job that I can do with my physical condition that I am in now.

Now that I'm learning how to read, I think there might be some jobs that might be opened up for me that I could use.

Chief's awareness of what he knows and doesn't know comes off as self-regulation. He embodies the turbulent flow of his opposing impulses, internalizing dominant expectations of what he should and should not know, what he can and cannot do; and as a result he feels bad and carries "hard feelings" with him. His comments reveal how Chief acted out his own autobiographical script and how he helped to maintain hegemony by keeping himself inscribed to a limited position because of his status as a nonliterate individual. Chief is Fanon's colonized black man who internalizes the discrimination that is imposed on him (*Black Skin* 98). His comments reveal frustration and disappointment; yet, in grappling with these conflicts, Chief also exhibits the qualities Fanon attributes to the person who resists his oppression. The desire for literacy is about the colonized person's desire to undo his colonization (see Chapter 6).

The desire to undo oppression is reminiscent of Spivak's advice to postmodern intellectuals—that to fairly critique subaltern experience, they must engage in "systemic unlearning" without "simply substituting the lost figure of the colonized" (295). Systemic unlearning involves a degree of self-critique that may be unattainable for traditional intellectuals (this is Spivak's argument). It is something I struggle with myself as an outsider to the community I research who knows primarily by trusting my participants' accounts. Their experience is not my experience. However, their experience carries a particular value that helps with the systemic unlearning I need to undergo if I am going to be an effective literacy worker standing under them. They offer me their theoretical perspectives on literacy, which exceed what people in more mainstream positions can know. The four authors are the experts on literacy and nonliteracy. The ways they theorize about literacy through their experience and their critique of material conditions can help us more thoroughly understand the relationship of literacy and power, its uses and abuses.

5

What Writing Enables

AS I'VE DEMONSTRATED IN PREVIOUS chapters, Read/Write/Now learners' relationship to writing is often fraught with frustration, anxiety, and bad memories. Learners grapple daily in their classes with the fear of not being able to get it—or get it right. They struggle with word order, sentence construction, and especially spelling. Often they resist writing because they claim it is too hard. The delight learners typically express over reading is less frequently voiced in regard to the process of writing even though they may be proud of their finished work. When I asked the participants how they use writing outside of Read/Write/Now, both George and Lee Ann initially made it clear that they write only to complete assignments at the center. Taking on the role of writer can be intimidating. While George and Lee Ann are both comfortable expressing their views orally, neither is prepared to present as a writer. Over the course of the study, however, their relationship to writing did shift. Their experiences at Read/Write/Now have taught them that there are multiple reasons for writing and that writing is something they can do; it is available to them when they need it.

For instance, George admitted that for a long time, even though he was getting more comfortable with the process of writing, he still didn't enjoy it, and that maybe reading is more important. His prioritizing of reading over writing suggests two things in general. First, reading may seem like a more important skill because it is the area in which nonliterate people have most obviously experienced a lack. Not being able to understand what culture puts out in print has most immediately oppressed them. Second, although everyone in the study agreed that they wanted to become better writers, the reasons why a person might need to write are less clear than those for why one should read. During one of our later interviews, George said this about his shifting relationship to writing: "Well, it [writing] seem a little bit better now. You know, because I don't seem, it don't feel like it's so much pressure anymore because . . . I just go ahead and do it, I guess [*laughs*]. If I have to do it, I just go ahead and do it. . . . It's not bad." By making writing ordinary, George has converted it into an everyday practice, one that he can execute without anxiety about his sense of self or his ability, similar to reading or using a computer. In this regard, George has transformed from someone who experienced writing as an activity that triggered feelings of incompetence and of being judged to someone who engages with writing as he would with any other aspect of learning. Although he produced quite a bit of new writing during the three subsequent years of my longitudinal research, George's enthusiasm for studying seemed to peter out. He continued to participate in class and to perfunctorily complete writing assignments, but he spoke longingly of leaving New England and returning to the South. By the time he decided to leave the center, George was done with this period of his life.

In contrast to George, who stayed at Read/Write/Now for nearly eight years, Lee Ann attended the program for just over a year. During this time, her few texts and her comments suggested that she was just beginning to think about how writing might be useful to her. She was ready to speak out about what she thought but not ready to use writing in other than prescribed ways.

Speaking out was clearly important to George and Lee Ann, but they did not yet view writing as the means to do this. Violeta and Chief, on the other hand, provide insights into the purposes writing can serve that are more difficult for George and Lee Ann to imagine. For people who have been marked as socially voiceless, acquiring new literacies can open up a space where they can achieve something they have wanted for a long time: to inscribe their views. Writing lends a different authority to their words because the words become permanent and, therefore, something that can be reread and contemplated repeatedly. Violeta has called this potential a "door open." For her, and for her peers, the acts of reflection and analysis through restorying their experiences in writing allow them to recognize aspects of their personal experience as matters of importance to a whole group and to transition from individual self-reflection and analysis toward broader social action. Flower observes that when people investigate the "story-behind-the-story," when they use writing to tell a different story that reveals what's going on beneath the surface (or common) narrative of their experience, they become able to share their "situated knowledge" (175). Making this knowledge public can influence not only the writer but also the audiences she reaches out to affect when her texts are circulated.

This chapter explores how Violeta and Chief turn their voices toward both personal action and social action through writing and thus create a version of the rhetorical agency Flower proposes, which I call textual agency. Exploring their purposes and processes of writing as a way to influence varying audiences can help us understand how the motivation to write is not always a function of—but may be for—the purpose of social action. The individual act of writing can become a move to communicate with varying external audiences. Because Violeta and Chief are strongly motivated by their desire to use literacy to recast the terms of their lives and to make changes outside of themselves, we can look at how their relationship to writing offers them a means of negotiating with the world. They can also model how writing helps people to develop a unique form of agency through their relationship to text.

In the process of writing, Violeta and Chief are able to "render" their experiences on the page, as Peter Elbow ("Reflections") and Anne Herrington argue: they can revise, reread, and analyze to recast the stories of their lives on their own terms. Self-narration is one way they assert themselves differently, but the process of writing permits them to do more than re-create experience through autobiographical narratives. As I explore in more depth in this chapter, writing makes it possible to reconceive of oneself as a subject. By writing in different situations and genres and directing their work to changing audiences, Violeta and Chief also rewrite their subjectivity. Actual moments of text production are sometimes instances when real time is suspended so that they can do the work of articulating thought through language. No one has taught Violeta or Chief how to render their experiences in writing, and yet the processes of reaching back to what they already know and then forward to what they believe or speculate are aspects of writing they both make use of in various contexts.

But Chief and Violeta don't stop there; rather, they help us see how people who are acquiring new literacies exercise the agency that writing can support—textual agency—when they use different genres and choose multiple options for distribution of their work. Chief and Violeta write to affect others with the hope that readers will contemplate their texts and be inspired to take action. As their comments suggest, writing can serve various purposes simultaneously, from enabling the kind of self-transformation that allows a person to change her position in society to encouraging others to speak out to counter hegemony. Through writing, they harness the turbulent flow of colliding discourses and redirect it toward their own purposes. They construct a desire for agency that is derived from their affectual desire to claim literacy and thereby present themselves as models for social action.

FROM SELF-TRANSFORMATION TO ACTION: WORDS FOR INVOKED AND SHIFTING AUDIENCES

In Chapter 4, I look at the process of restorying one's experiences and how that offers possibilities for defining self differently. Particularly when restorying is enacted through writing, it offers the author opportunities to cast her self and her interactions in the world on her own terms. The work of restorying allows for an articulation of self-knowledge that the writer makes permanent and can revisit; thus, a writer's experiences can be lived again. Some critical educators believe that self-transformation is a necessary stage of critical awareness leading to social action. Giroux, for example, understands the individual as transitioning from self-transformation to critical action (*Border Crossings*, "Literacy"). This conception of empowerment through literacy necessitates that one's goal be Freirean praxis: "the action of men and women upon their world in order to transform it" (Freire, *Pedagogy* 79). Writing then becomes a deliberate means of countering oppressive forces with the clear intent of effecting change. While I don't believe there is a distinct path toward critical action, I have noticed that the four authors' moves toward critical action began with self-awareness. Chief and Violeta both harness writing as a means to claim personal and social agency. Later in this chapter, I examine how Chief uses writing to reach out to actual public audiences. Chief knows his voice and how he wants to use it. In this section, I focus on Violeta, for whom writing is always a means of being and becoming.

Violeta develops textual agency through the process of writing in different situations and for different audiences. The same piece of writing can be invented in various contexts, thus altering the rhetorical event. Violeta composed certain texts with either a teacher or a relative in mind as her initial audience, but over time she was offered new forums for sharing those texts. When she changed the context for which the text was intended, the audience was altered, and as a result, her relationship to that audience also shifted. The generative act of writing, and the shifts writing takes as it is respun for new purposes, audiences, and occasions, allow Violeta to reposition herself within her texts, enabling self-transformation.

Violeta reflects on the letter she wrote to her son who is in prison in Puerto Rico. She claimed at first to have composed it as an effort to make amends and to articulate herself in written English (see Chapter 3). Here is the letter again:

> Dear Miguel,
> The reason I am writing this letter is because I love you very much. Please don't get in trouble any more. Remember God is all the time with you. I know you are now in the wrong place. You didn't do the right thing. My dear son, I think about you all the time. I hope you have learned the right way now.
> I am going to P.R. this summer. I would like to see you doing excellent in your life. Remember you have children.

When your children ask about your life, what answer are you going to have for you children? I will feel better if you try to do something nice in your life. When you do the right thing you will feel proud. This is my little letter for you. I hope when you get this letter you feel good. God bless you.

Love,
Mom

But then she also has this to say about her purposes for writing:

Um, I wrote this letter for my son because I know it's a lot of mother in this world, it's the same way that happened in the life like me. It's only not me. When, you know, some children coming and giving you a hard time in your life, and you try the best thing in life. I know I'm not the one; I'm not the only mother that's happened. And sometimes some mother, it's very hard for her. I understand that. Maybe some mother, they can see this, and they say, "See, she did it. I can do it." Or I give them like an example, example or something that a mother can start it with the son to write it, a letter. *Porque*, it's a lot of mothers in the world that have their son in jail. And some time they so sad, so angry, they want it, they want to read it, they want to write a letter, and they don't know how to start it. They don't know how to say, how to explain to their son, or they afraid. And I want this: all the mothers in the world, they can see this and they say: "See, she did it. I can make it too."

Violeta's experiences as a single parent, a Puerto Rican woman, and a literacy learner converge in the letter that she produced and mailed to her son, but composing the letter, mailing it, and reaching out to make changes in her life are not her sole purposes for writing. There's something else too. In addition to developing herself as a more literate person, Violeta might be able to use her knowledge to inspire and educate others, especially single mothers in situations like hers. Her experience is common; other mothers also suffer as she does. Violeta knows their suffering, empathizes with them, and she can offer single mothers a model based on the wisdom she has gained in the process of her own self-examination. Violeta has transformed her self as a subject through her literacy education, and now she can reach out from her altered position to affect others. Her pattern of using her own experience as a source of personal knowledge and then recontextualizing it as a learning model for others demonstrates how people sometimes reconstruct their life stories as a way to communicate what they know about education and the world around them.

The move to imagine a different audience beyond her son and herself means that Violeta no longer frames her situation as solely personal but rather as an issue that may be pertinent to new and larger audiences. She reconceives the issue as something outside of herself that she can critique and, through her writing, attempt to change. She can also attempt to change the way others understand the issue. When she repositions herself in relation to the letter, Violeta is doing something social for the benefit of others. In the act of writing and circulating it to others, the purpose of the letter changes. What begins as a personal letter with the aim of repairing a relationship and persuading her son to make better choices—shifts. When the audience broadens from her son to single mothers,

from a single real recipient to unlimited imagined others, Violeta also changes. She consciously alters her own subjectivity in relation to her own writing. Now she turns herself into a spokesperson. As her authorial position shifts, so does her relationship to the writing itself. The personal letter transforms into an example for single mothers of the type of situation they might be expected to confront, and Violeta transforms herself into a model narrator. By writing the letter and later reconceiving her relationship to it, Violeta alters the entire rhetorical situation.

In an essay titled "The Single Mother," Violeta took a more explicit step to address outside audiences. When I asked her who besides herself (and perhaps her intimate acquaintances) she imagined reaching with her narrative, she was emphatic: "Every single, every single mom. . . . What I tell every single mom, that I can say to the mom is: 'I know it's hard. Very hard.' Sometime mom will say, 'Oh, I give up! I can't do it. It's not, it's not.'" But Violeta does not believe that giving up is an option. When she writes, Violeta performs a certain way; the writing then circulates among others (or potential others). The same written performance circulates among various audiences with varying effects. So for Violeta, writing is not only about telling her story; it is also about the way she chooses to prepare her narrative to become a document that might be read and reread.

The Single Mother

The mother works hard when she is a single mother. She has to work even harder when she has a lot of children. She is mother and father and she has to take care of the house. When there are problems coming, she has to fix them. She feels like everything is so hard because when she fixes the problems, another is coming. When the bills come, she has to pay them. She has to buy the clothes and the food. Sometimes she does not have time for herself.

For example, I am in school now because my mother never put me in school. My life was very hard. It is hard for me because I do not know about reading and writing. I was afraid to make mistakes. Sometimes, I am so afraid to talk with people. Sometimes, I feel very confused. I do so much work with my kids in my house. We have to keep everything in order. I will never give up in my life.

In "The Single Mother," as in the letter to her son, Violeta uses her experience as an example of learning how to cope with difficult situations. Her interview comments show that she has been aware for quite a while that writing can be used for more than reflection and self-analysis. By imagining and invoking new audiences, Violeta can rewrite her own experience and also reinterpret the cultural experiences of others like her. Herrington notes that rendering experience in writing includes "rendering vicariously" when one imagines a situation (238). What is transformative for Violeta is not just that she can use writing to reflect on her experiences; she can also imagine and invoke new audiences because she can create a rhetorical situation that repositions her. It doesn't necessarily matter whether the audience is actual or imagined, because every audience offers Violeta opportunities to transform herself.

Writing helps Violeta shift her subject position in relation to her own experience and to others. In "The Single Mother," her stated goals are to speak out on behalf of single mothers and encourage them to get an education. As Violeta imagines this text circulating among more distant readers, she envisions her words motivating others to be strong, to endure their struggles as single mothers, and to resist their social positioning. Violeta tests out an image she has created of herself as an advocate and a fighter both for her own benefit and the benefit of potential others.

Violeta's sense of herself as someone who is in a state of becoming and who can imagine her writing addressing different audiences suggests that it is possible for the roles of writer and audience to shift in relation to each other.[1] By making choices concerning audience, Violeta alters her own subjectivity. Playing with audience becomes a vehicle through which to rewrite herself. Barbara Biesecker's concept of audience helps to explain how this transformation occurs. Biesecker explains that "if rhetorical events are analysed from within the thematic of *différance*, it becomes possible to read discursive practices neither as rhetorics directed to preconstituted and known audiences nor as rhetorics 'in search of' objectively identifiable but yet undiscovered audiences" (126). When she writes, Violeta rewrites herself. She writes herself for new audiences. The new audiences and situations Violeta creates are not simply imaginary. Her writing is not a fantasy. Rather, she is engaging in the very real work of inventing an audience in relation to the subject she creates in her writing. As she repositions herself, she repositions her audience as well. Violeta's writing may not circulate much, but what matters more is that when she writes Violeta allows herself to alter her subjectivity. Writing creates the conditions of possibility for Violeta to gain agency.

"The Single Mother" does more than simply inspire other mothers. It reaches back to Violeta's own social position, and it also attempts to revise dominant literacy narratives by offering an alternative. Violeta works to rewrite her own life as well as the larger narrative. Notice the shift in focus from the first to the second paragraph. While the first paragraph addresses the situation of single mothers in general, in the second paragraph Violeta constructs herself as someone who is consciously making changes by learning how to read and write. She presents herself as a woman who used to be afraid and disempowered but who is now taking active charge by getting an education.

I asked Violeta why she decided to write "The Single Mother" as an example for others:

> I decided like a example because I have a lot of children. Some mom have a lot of children. They stuck out in a house: "Oh, I cannot go, I have a lot of children. How I going to make it with children and how go to school?" It's not. You can make it. You can go. . . . When the kids in school, you can do it. . . . You can do it at the same time. And you know what? And the children see you: "Oh, my mami's going to school. My mom wants she diploma to get her GED. See my mom's do it, I can do it too. Let me follow my mom. . . . Look at my ma; she's going to go too. She can do it, just go straight away this going mom." . . . I share my goals. *To everybody.* I sit down with [my daughter]: "Look what Mom do in school." And

when I do something in school, and I tell the teacher, "Give me the copy." I like a little girl, so happy, and I share it to my children!

Violeta wants her children to see her as someone inspired by education, but she also makes it clear that her audience is not limited; she is repositioning herself as someone who can speak to "everybody" about inequity. Violeta's narratives address not merely her own life but also larger problems of single motherhood and public schooling, both extremely public issues. By confronting these issues for the benefit of a broad, albeit invoked, audience, Violeta is attempting to alter the discourse that has inscribed her into a particular social position.

While Violeta does not literally circulate her text to her imagined audiences, she is responding to shifts in the rhetorical situation itself. When she envisioned the letter to her son as a model to inspire single mothers, she assigned it new meaning. Only after she had written the letter, when she imagined its potential to affect others, did she reconceive her purpose. The letter transformed from a personal piece into an example of how single mothers could speak back to the conditions of single motherhood. In this way, the self-transformation Violeta gains from writing a letter becomes social action. Imagining circulating her text to various audiences provides Violeta with opportunities to relate to her own writing in new ways. If she is writing for the purpose of social action, then imagining increasing her circulation networks makes it possible to inspire more people to consider her ideas.

Violeta already knows about critical literacy. Now she is writing back to culture. Thus, literacy becomes the vehicle for her to theorize about inequity as she confronts it in her writing. When she writes, Violeta allows herself to perform a kind of restorying of conditions in her life that is her way of theorizing; when she recasts her experiences in writing, giving herself a certain narrative power and control that she might not have had in an earlier moment, she is also theorizing about how inequity has affected her and people like her, and she is using the situation of writing to disrupt that oppression.

Violeta imagines herself on a bus with Rosa Parks. This fictional situation begins as an assignment during a project on the Civil Rights Movement. She takes Carolyn's assignment and inserts herself into it. Violeta identifies with a strong leader as a way to make herself strong and to reflect on the lives of other women. Once again, as I mention in Chapter 4, she puts herself into the role of spectator of her own experience (Britton) by using writing to give herself distance for reflection and analysis. Here we witness the transformative power that writing holds for Violeta. She uses the space of writing to restory herself as a woman who can stand up to injustice and "never give up." She turns herself into a resister.

My Conversation with Rosa Parks
Violeta Blanca

One day I had a dream that I was sitting next to Rosa parks on bus. I said, I am proud of you because you never gave up. You are a strong woman. You helped the black people to not be segregated. You helped the black people understand why it is important to vote. You decided to bring the people together to make a protest. You helped get justice to the black people. The white people were prejudiced to the black people. Thank you for your story because we learned about your good work.

Rather than simply refer to the event that makes Parks famous, Violeta acknowledges, by writing her own story, the strength of a woman who had the courage to act on behalf of others. We talk about the way she constructs Rosa Parks:

> LAUREN: Okay, in this one you say, "One day I had a dream that I was sitting next to Rosa Parks on [the] bus." And I was wondering, was it, was it really? Did you really dream that? Or did you . . . was it like fiction? Were you making it up?
>
> VIOLETA: Uh huh, making it up, fiction. At the time, well, we picked out that one, and I was getting in my head, you know, like, um, like a movie. You know, and I start to write it. . . . I'm magic, you know. I see how she, how that

happen. And sometime we talking about story, we get it in our head, and I think, oh she was like that. I knew how she was. I think she was like that. That's the kind of imagination that you have in your head. You know I'm a lived that part. When we really find a story, like, you *live* that part. And I say, oh my, you see she dress like that, you know, we use all that detail. That's what I mean. . . .

L: Now, maybe I'm just connecting these because they're one after the other [order of papers in Violeta's portfolio]— but, do you think Rosa Parks is like a single mother? In the way she's strong?

V: Uh, I think the way she's strong is because it was bad thing that happen in her life. And she never gave up. You know, she keeping going. And I think she just the kind of person, when she wants something, she going the right way: "That's what I want, I want to learn." She never gave up, she front of everybody that was accusing her, she go, "This is what I want, this is the kind of person that I am. And right here, I want to do this, and I want to do it." This is a strong woman, like, um, you know, um, something happen in the life of the woman, and the woman say, "Ah, no more! That's it. I give up." No. She not. And I feel proud about that. She keep on moving her life.

Violeta creates an image for herself, based on the way she imagines Rosa Parks, of a strong woman she wants to become. To become that woman, she needs to keep moving, keep interrogating the situations she is in without allowing those situations to overpower her. By repositioning herself as a resister, instead of as the woman who was afraid of being in public, Violeta re-creates herself as a figure who confronts the limit-situations of poverty, single motherhood, and nonliteracy. For her, an important step in countering the turbulent flow of oppressive situations is to imagine herself into the position she wants to embody, in this case acting in the guise of Parks. The woman Violeta conjures as Rosa Parks is herself, a woman who has had a difficult life yet is able to articulate: "That's what I want. I want to learn."

In Violeta's imaginary dream, she situates herself on a bus where she and Parks are strong together. When we talk about this piece, Violeta describes herself as "magic" because the writing process enabled her to imagine what Parks might be thinking. The authors in this study generally do not experience writing as holding a magical means of connection or insight (Elbow, "Writing and Magic"; Johnson); however, in her description of composing the essay, Violeta talks explicitly about this sense of her own magic. She describes the sense of "knowing" that legitimizes fiction, and she shows that writing offers her the possibility of making a leap through "the kind of imagination that you have in your head." Violeta does a wonderful job of describing the experience of imagining how someone else thinks. Her statement is also inspiring because of the confidence she expresses when she describes her ability to get inside the fictional Parks's head and know her. Violeta believes in her own ability to connect with her writing subjects and be transformed along with them.

Her gestures of resistance exemplify the kind of activism that Elizabeth Flynn, Patricia Sotirin, and Ann Brady call "feminist resilience." Although Violeta often works from her imagination, her writing is an act of being and becoming. Her texts are intended to reach out and affect others. This type of movement and intentionality is exactly what characterizes feminist resilience. Violeta's activism is community oriented, reflecting her inner strength as she copes with the daily difficulties of living and reaches out to influence women in like situations.

The textual agency that Violeta gains as a writer of these texts may not change the world; nonetheless, it is a form of action. Altering her subject position as she does here will have an impact in the future. As we see at the end of this chapter, changing her subjectivity inspires additional forms of social action that Violeta engages in later. Textual agency, which strengthens as it is connected to the act of composing and sharing one's texts, is unique to writing. It reflects the individual recursive process of reflecting, analyzing, rendering (Elbow, "Reflections"; Herrington), and restorying, in combination with the more social aspect of extending beyond oneself to affect potential readers. Writing can be simultaneously transformative for social and public purposes as well as personal ones—purposes that cannot be separated. Public audience and circulation are part of the way writing functions for self-transformation. In writing, Violeta can reposition herself as a Parks-like fighter, a strong woman whose lived experiences have motivated her to tell a different story that can serve as a model for other women. Similarly, in "The Single Mother," Violeta constructs herself as a spokesperson who can advise others through writing so that they might act for social change.

FROM SELF-REALIZATION TO SOCIAL TRANSFORMATION: WORDS FOR THE PUBLIC

Unlike Violeta, Chief takes an authoritative stance in all of his writing, assuming the responsibility of educating readers whether he is writing to a broad general audience to inform them about an issue or to an intimate audience that is learning about the pain he keeps hidden. By reaching out to broad audiences through multiple genres of writing, Chief is able to circulate views that he used to feel were quieted because he was not literate enough to speak out ("my opinion don't mean nothing here"). He did not feel this way because he didn't know what he thought but because he didn't have the right words to express his opinions to others. Learning to read and write better has helped Chief to become more confident about voicing his opinions. Now when Chief writes, he is demonstrating that he does have the proper words. He can inscribe those words indelibly on a page where others can read them and where he can reflect on them. The permanence of writing provides Chief with textual agency. Writing has also allowed him to transcend the shyness that kept him silent in the past (see Chapter 2). Now Chief can use writing to inform other people so that they too will question the ways they are socially positioned. Thus, Chief, like Violeta, uses his notions of audience to revise his own subjectivity, but rather than altering his relationship to his experience, he alters his sense of how his voice might be used to help others.

Typically Chief relates to writing by establishing an audience and then setting up situations in which he can experiment with his subject position. For example, when he wrote to learners at Read/ Write/Now as newsletter editor, he was able to give himself the authority of the editor who was addressing his readers. Though his audience was real, he was using the rhetorical event to experiment with himself as the subject. Usually Chief takes a spectator's position to address his self. He reflects on himself from a distance, observing his own experiences and actions, even in his introspective writing.

I see Violeta and Chief moving beyond the need to validate their own experience toward a larger imperative to reach out to others for social transformation. By writing in different genres, addressing various audiences, and circulating their texts publicly, they are able to position themselves for social transformation. The agency they gain through the production of texts allows them to bridge personal, public, and social goals and rewrite both their individual scripts and dominant discourses. They are writing to change conditions not only for themselves but also for others whom their writing might reach. Their most significant readers may be people like themselves, nonliterate people and others who are acquiring new literacies, those whose voices have been silenced. By telling their stories of nonliteracy, Violeta and Chief achieve one of the objectives Chief articulates later in this chapter—putting on the page stories that have not been told before, at least not from the perspective of those who have been labeled "illiterate." That is one level of their social action. They write to their peers and to others like them, and their writing circulates via program-wide publications and informal sharing. However, their social action is no less significant when the audience is small and familiar.

Chief

In the previous section, I concentrated on how Violeta relates to writing. For her, the move to social action is always connected to the personal; her experiences prompt her to consider new contexts for writing and for action. Altering her subjectivity is one of her primary motivations for writing. But for Chief, the motivation to write is different. He does not write to find out who he is or to change his self. In his remarks in Chapter 4, he makes it clear that he does not see increasing his literacy as a change in self: "I never want to change. I want to be myself. But when I say, when I speak of bettering myself it means, better—learn better how to read. And, uh, speech. And, uh, using proper words. That's what I mean by better myself. But physically, I'm going to stay me." Instead, Chief uses writing as a way to spread the word about what he knows. When he alters experience, it is so that *others* will be affected.

Writing in a variety of genres with awareness of how he can affect different readers is one way Chief works toward social transformation. In the persuasive piece "Jim Crow is Expelled from School," Chief demonstrates how he took an event that was meaningful to him personally and significant for his community and retold it so that it could serve new purposes. Chief tells a story for the benefit of the public while also working through painful experiences from his past. This illustrates Chief's desire to use writing to call attention to stories from his lived experience that may have been previously untold while creating a particular subject position that protects his identity. He is able to achieve multiple purposes at once.

Jim Crow is Expelled from School

I know how the people of Clarendon County South Carolina felt in 1947, when a good friend of mine came to me and said, "Chief I am going to sue Clarendon County school board." Ruben James and I sat and we talked about it. I must say that at first it made me a little nervous. We talked about our families and about our farms. We knew it would be hard. Then we talked about equal rights. We worried about our families being threatened. Finally, Ruben said, "Chief talk to some of the other families in Clarendon County." To our surprise there were other families who felt the same way we did. Ruben, the other families and I had a meeting and we decided since Ruben came up with the idea, the lawsuit should be named Ruben James versus Clarendon County.

And as soon as the lawsuit began trouble began. Ruben couldn't get help with his farm. The businesses wouldn't sell him supplies.

In 1948, my friend, Ruben James, had more bad luck. The court threw out Ruben's case. That summer, Ruben couldn't get help to harvest his crop. We had to sit and watch his oats, beans, and wheat rot in the fields. But we would not give up.

In March 1949, Ruben and I, along with a small group of farmers, traveled to South Carolina State capital. In Columbia, we met a lawyer by the name of Thurgood Marshall, an African American who worked for the National Association for the Advancement of Colored People. We talked to Marshall about the injustices to our children. Marshall said nothing. When the meeting was over he said, "We must fight this battle together." He said they needed to find 20 more people who are willing to sue. And once Thurgood Marshall had the 20 people together, we sued the school board of Clarendon County.

By Chief Dawson

The events that Chief reports on actually took place in his home county in South Carolina and became part of one of the four cases that combined into *Brown v. Board of Education*. Chief took this story about a locally famous desegregation case and inserted himself into it, similar to the way Violeta put herself on a bus with Rosa Parks. Although Chief was really about seven years old at the time, by claiming the situation as his own story and literally transforming himself into a participant in a historical event, he could reflect on the experience as if he had been there. Fiction enabled Chief to position himself as a leader who "knows how the people felt" and to tell a story of his own history with racial politics. The tactics he uses for writing about an important historical event, including overlaying his own experience onto it, allow him to make a move toward social action. By fictionalizing the narrative, Chief can educate people who read his story about an important period in history, and he can rewrite his own script by contextualizing it in terms of racial history. He employs a narrative genre because it helps highlight his connection to his community. Community realities are his realities. The past is present in how he understands his relationship to his community. The events that took place in Clarendon County are embodied in Chief's experiences. By crafting the narrative in this way, he embodies the past in such a way that he makes the past present for his readers. Chief highlights this important historical event that he believes will grab people's attention, and then he gives himself an activist role.

He talks about why and how he wrote the narrative and why it is important to him to share his knowledge with outside readers:

> This was about the segregation down in the South. And, uh, this is the kind of stuff I grew up to. . . . That's something I can relate with, so when we're writing it—this was pretty hard on me, because bringing up—it was bringing back a lot of memories and stuff. . . . She [Melissa] wanted me to tell my part of it, so I told it like if it was me and him working together. . . . Well, it was—it's his story, but I grew up in the—I wasn't in that down there with him, but I grew up down there, and I was going through the same thing he was going through. . . . It's a fiction. . . . She [Melissa] said . . . , "If you was going to write about this story, how would you do it?" And then, so, you, you would, say he was your friend. So that's how I got started. So, I wrote like me and him was working together. Getting people together. . . . This story was sort of hard. It was sort of touching too because if you never, if you never lived this life, you—the people—don't know about it. A lot of people don't even know what a sharecropper is.

Fiction allows the story to become Chief's in the same way that he implies it belongs to all the people of Clarendon County. Because of that, there is no conflict for Chief in telling a historical narrative as if he were present. In this piece, as in much of his writing, Chief positions himself as a leader in order to guide others in identifying with his point of view. He even explains that Melissa adjusted her assignment to suit him and encouraged him to tell about this case as though he had been present. "I was supposed to write like being a leader," Chief explains.

What really happened to Ruben James?

Ruben here, this guy, after he done all of this and got his people together, he lost his farm, you know. And they wouldn't sell him nothing and there wouldn't nobody give him no more credit, so he, he, he stuck his neck out. In real life, he lost everything. I don't know if, I don't know the government, even the government didn't help him. . . . Well, well, it's, lot of peoples, lot of that stuff down there was kept hush-mouth.

Chief's writing, combined with his comments, illustrate the experience of being silenced by explicit racism. He describes how the school segregation that was common when he was a boy operated similarly to the way Ruben James and his neighbors were discredited:

They didn't want nobody, they wouldn't want nobody to know that they was doing, uh, doing peoples like that. And, uh, schools, they, uh, the whites had these nice schools and everything nice in them. And we had to take their hand-me-down books. They didn't want to buy us books for our school. They wanted to put black people to never be able to read so they would never learn how to do what they wanted—tried to keep them down all the time.

This idea of people being kept "hush-mouth" repeats in Chief's more controversial narratives. He deliberately points to the ways African Americans have been silenced and shamed. Chief's story reflects on the condition of being kept "hush-mouth" and on how the people of Clarendon County resisted their subaltern positioning by taking action. By writing this story, he continues the process of confronting an oppressive position and using writing to change it. When he retells the situation, he is able to make it more public and inform more people about the racial politics of South Carolina in the 1940s and 1950s. As someone who envisions himself as a spokesperson for the people, Chief takes responsibility for making sure that people know. For Chief and people in his community, becoming more literate means earning the right to "do what they wanted" and to take charge of their own subjectivity. This is how

Chief theorizes about racial politics and how the people can unite to effect change.

In his longest piece, "This Story is About Violence," Chief writes in typical fashion to analyze a situation for the purpose of informing and educating others. He composed this news report a few years prior to my study for a program-wide publication on domestic violence. I assume he had assistance with editing and typing at the time he wrote it. I include it here for a few reasons, one of which is that Chief was the only learner at Read/Write/Now who submitted a piece of writing addressing the topic of abuse of men by women. He is not afraid to take an unpopular position in his writing and to argue for what he knows is important. He is also unafraid to experiment with genre. In "This Story is About Violence," Chief has made a deliberate decision about how best to report a controversial subject to the public.

This Story is About Violence

There is a lot of violence and abuse in the world today. We hear about women and children being abused. But, what about men? There are a lot of men being abused. When a woman or a child has been abused, we hear about it on TV or in the newspaper. But when a man is abused we don't hear too much about it because he's ashamed or he doesn't want anyone to know he's been abused.

Some men put up with abusive women because they love the woman or they have children and he doesn't want to leave his children. A man's pride keeps him from telling anyone. The woman knows he won't tell anyone so that makes the woman more aggressive. She knows her man or her husband won't report her to the authorities.

I know a woman who used to beat up her husband. She was always hitting on him. He would throw up his hands and walk away. He knew that if he left her, his kids wouldn't be treated right. Here is another story about a man being abused. The man left his wife and moved in with a friend. The man moved out because his wife would throw stuff at him, swear at him and was also cheating on him. So the man was at his friend's house and the wife came by. They wouldn't let her in. Half of the door was glass that she broke out, reached in, and unlocked the door! When she got in she was screaming and yelling. The guy was going to call the police on her—but the husband told her to leave. He didn't call the police because he did not want her to go to jail for the kid's sake.

When we hear about abuse, the first thing we think about is someone beating someone. But that is not always true. When there is abuse it doesn't always have to be about physical fighting. There are other ways to abuse. I have a friend who worked two jobs. His wife did not work. She would nag him and wouldn't have his food prepared for him to go to his other job. She knew he only had enough time to walk in, and change his clothes before he was off to his second job. He didn't even have time to eat at home. He had to take his food with him and yet she didn't prepare food for him because she wanted to torture him. They had three children and she knew he loved his children and he wouldn't leave them. So she took advantage of him. She kept nagging, bossing him around, swearing at him, etc. She knew he loved his children and wouldn't do anything about it. He had too much pride to tell us about it, so he didn't talk about it.

When we hear about domestic violence don't think it is just about women and children. There are a lot of men being abused too. Abuse and violence are a big problem in the world today. We hear about it on TV, in the paper and on the radio. We have to find a way to stop it.

Chief wrote this piece knowing that the Read/Write/Now community would read it. He tells it from the perspective of a journalist speaking to the public, as he often does when he writes something news related. His genre choices make it clear that Chief is aware of how genre can enable different voices and positions, as his interview comments reveal. His purpose here was "to get their attention. You wanted to get their attention. . . . And you, uh, you never hear about men's, no talk about men abuse, about men abused, right? . . . But they do be. And, and, I tell you, down like this, it's about the first time you ever see something like this on paper." The news report is the most appropriate genre for getting people to pay attention. Chief also selects it because of the authoritative tone he can assume as a journalist reporting. In this way, he sets himself up to convey what he considers an unpopular perspective. Chief has described himself as a "news freak," and so it makes sense that he would feel compelled to speak out on an issue that he believes has gone unrecognized in the news. His comments demonstrate how much it matters to him personally to inform the public about issues that have been kept quiet, in this case by the media and by "proud" men. He takes on the journalistic imperative to put the story on paper for "the first time."

By putting it on paper for the first time, Chief also takes responsibility for releasing the story to the public. Informing people about something he believes they need to know, and making that news permanent, matters a great deal to him. Chief is speaking back to the "shyness" he experienced when he was nonliterate. In the past, he kept his opinions to himself because of his anxiety that others would view him as not having an opinion that mattered. But in the guise of a reporter who can insist that his story is important, he can undo the shyness of his former self. Although I see Chief using writing primarily as a means to get his voice out there so that others can act, underlying this motivation is the desire to revise his subjectivity. He has turned himself into a spokesperson with the authority to encourage others to act based on his words.

Many of Chief's strengths as a writer are exhibited here. He uses the news report to construct a complex argument that contains three embedded examples of men who have been abused by their wives ("I know a woman . . . ," "Here is another story . . . ," "I have a friend . . ."). This form allows him to construct an argument with multiple parts that appeals to a large audience.

When I asked him about his motivations for writing this narrative, Chief explained that he knew most people at Read/Write/Now would be writing about abuse of women and children, but nobody would represent the position of men. He knew he had to write this piece, which, he said, just poured out once he got started.

The following section of an interview transcript begins where Chief has been discussing how familiar the public is with the issue of abuse of women and children, whereas abuse of men is generally unreported.

> LAUREN: You're taking that story that people are supposed to be quiet about, and you're putting it out there.
>
> CHIEF: I'm letting them know that it's, it's abuse be going both ways; it's not just a one-way street.
>
> L: So why is it so important for you? Why do you think you can do that? Speak out like that? Why isn't somebody else speaking out?
>
> C: Well, I, I, because I really am, uh, a lot of what I'm saying here is about myself—about my first wife. I took a lot of punishment from her, and I took a lot of grout [flack]. I lost, I had a brand-new, I had a beautiful brand-new brick home down South, and I had to give that up on account of her. I bought a brick home before I moved up here. I wasn't but seventeen years old, and I was buying my own home. And my house could have been—and I— it was right in, in the neighborhood where a lot of my schoolmates was down there, and I had to lose my house. I was so embarrassed, I had to—That's when I came up here because I didn't want to, uh, let my friends know that I had to give up my house because—and they, they got theirs.
>
> L: So, it's like the story had to get, held, kept quiet for so long.
>
> C: Yeah. This had a lot to do with me writing this like this. . . . I was putting some of me into this story.

An autobiographical urgency finally surfaces in our conversation that surprises me. I hadn't realized that under his journalistic guise, Chief was reporting on his own situation. By representing men who have been silenced, he was able to tell his own story. He wanted to call attention to the issue without making the narrative explicitly autobiographical. In another section of our interview, Chief discussed how he had considered writing an article on the same topic for the Read/Write/Now newsletter but decided against it because he did not want people to know that he was telling his own story. The journalistic form permitted him to externalize the issue as an argument. By making these decisions about genre and how to present himself, Chief demonstrates just how savvy he is as a writer. He made these rhetorical choices on his own without asking a teacher for advice about which genre to use or how to craft the story.

"This Story is About Violence" exemplifies how Chief has taught himself to use writing for social transformation. His interview comments also reveal what the text does not: that his purposes are not separated. He writes with the dual goals of educating others and reworking his own experience. Thus, writing gives Chief a means to reposition himself in relation to painful experiences, simultaneous with turning those experiences into models for public contemplation. Without naming the experience as his own, Chief uses the news report to inform people about abuse so that they can then act on it. His dual purpose of rewriting his experience and using his experiences to encourage others to act is only possible in writing. And the way Chief makes his autobiography implicit while framing a public issue as explicit is a complex rhetorical move.

Writing also enables Chief to take his sense of himself as a leader to another level where he can use writing for social transformation. He achieves both self- and social transformation simultaneously because he can reenvision himself while maintaining his privacy as he revises for a different audience. This move toward social transformation occurs when Chief circulates his story to a nonimmediate audience, even when this audience is other people in the program at Read/Write/Now. He aims his narrative toward public audiences with the expectation that his words will encourage others to think about abuse and take action because his text has affected them, thereby placing his audience in the role of potential activists. He, like Violeta, is enacting the resilience that leads to change. When Chief encourages others to act critically, he is engaging in Freirean praxis, in which reflection and action go hand in hand.

Chief already understands that he can use his public voice to change things to the extent that Daniel Mahala and Jody Swilky claim: storytelling can be "a powerful challenge to dominant ways of knowing" (384). He knows that his voice can make people think about their subjectivity, just as it has made him think about his own. Writing gives him that opportunity to perform other ways of thinking that can challenge dominant discourses. It also allows Chief to call attention to matters of importance. He typically uses writing to situate himself in new positions where he can act as an advocate. Yet reaching out to local audiences and occasionally to larger publics is only the beginning of Chief's social activism. His goal of being a leader includes extending himself to gain greater circulation networks. When he circulates his texts among new audiences, Chief achieves something else: he changes the context in which his texts are received.

Chief reaches out to two audiences; one is the immediate readership of people at Read/Write/Now. But Chief also suggests that others outside of the center may read his work. Sometimes he does physically circulate his writing in more public contexts. Whether he actually makes this move or not, he still assumes the position of an editor who expects that the public will be reading his work. The process of writing allows Chief to invoke more than one audience simultaneously. This move to address multiple audiences is not only possible but also necessary, as a writer (particularly a news writer) does not always know what circulation routes his text will take.

For Chief, changing his audience and repositioning himself in relation to it allow him to expand the range of his rhetorical actions, moves that Biesecker would argue are possible when one considers the subject as a being in flux who changes in relation to his audience and purpose. For example, when Chief distributed his newsletters at his sister's church in Allentown, Pennsylvania, he was no longer addressing a known or necessarily supportive audience. He made a deliberate decision to circulate his writing among another audience because he was confident in his own voice and the message he had to share with the public. Chief, as the writing subject, remains attached to his ideas on the importance of literacy education; and by circulating the newsletters to more distant, larger audiences, he sends those ideas off into the world, hoping they will have an effect. Repositioning the audience allows him to experiment with the text itself. When Chief's analysis of his own experience and his public advocacy come together, he becomes able to write for the purpose of social transformation.

When he was editor of the *Read/Write/Now Daily News,* Chief consciously addressed his audience for the purpose of social transformation. In one early letter, he wrote,

Chief Your Editor

Dear Students and Staff

For the last six months we enjoy working with the Read/Write/Now Daily News it has been a very Educational for me to learn the editing skills. And the more I work the more I want to work with the paper I enjoy trying to answear your questions so keep up the good works I enjoy reading your stories the Amazing little Girl. By Millie Ramos and the story writing to Email Fiends By Monique Taylor. She said and He said and that the good part about being the Editor of a Read/Write/Now Daily News paper.

Chief focuses on himself as editor, reflecting in his usual fashion on what he enjoys about his position. Highlighting his own experience is intended to persuade others to follow his example. He also makes it clear that part of his enjoyment is in connecting with the people and reading their work ("I enjoy trying to answear your questions so keep up the good works I enjoy reading your stories"). While Chief is musing on the pleasure of being editor, he does so in a way that includes readers in his experience as he encourages them to contribute to the paper. His words encourage them to participate and become as active in their education as he is. Chief shows how he transitions from a state of self-transformation to a position where he can take other people along with him.

Violeta

During the period of the study, Violeta only imagined possibilities of distribution, but a couple of years later she turned these imaginings into reality. She left Read/Write/Now for a while because of child care demands, yet she remained in contact and eventually "stopped back in." During her absence, Violeta participated in a project to educate the Latino community in Springfield about the effects of HIV. She had been involved in producing a DVD that she hoped would be an inspiration to single mothers like her. The completed DVD was shown at a conference in Boston, and Violeta spoke at the event. Although Violeta did not do this work at Read/Write/Now, she went out into the world, where she participated in making a film, wrote, and spoke publicly, interacting with actual public audiences.

Her involvement in creating the text and images for the DVD and then presenting them to outside audiences demonstrate that Violeta has continued to push her words beyond personal experience to influence broader communities. Her audiences have become actualized through her ongoing desire to engage with people to express the words that she believes must be said. Through her writing—and now in film and speech—she has upheld her commitment to advocate for herself and for others, using her literacy as a means to connect with increasingly public, distant audiences.

The DVD was created as part of a project called TOLD: Telling Our Legacies Digitally. Violeta remembers that when she was asked to contribute she was "excited" to help the "woman Latina." She reflected in an interview that sometimes a woman gets "depressed"; sometimes she thinks, "I'm going to die. But she's not." The DVD was originally intended for an audience of Springfield's North End community members, and in her narrative Violeta speaks passionately to viewers about her will to keep moving through her life. When she tells her story, Violeta continually gives thanks to God; she also reflects on her own decisions about how to shape her life.[2]

In the transcript and in our subsequent interview, Violeta expresses a new theme that wasn't apparent in her earlier writing or interviews. Now she talks about her desire to educate herself about medications and treatments by reading news articles and journals.

She is taking a more active stance in confronting her own illness through literacy. In the DVD transcript (translated from Spanish), she comments: "I participated in meetings, and I learned more every day. About the medications. And this gave me more motivation to continue living."

When I interview Violeta about the DVD, I am struck by a definite shift in her subject position. She explains that now she speaks with her doctors and counselors about medications and treatments that are available, and she requests the literature about them. She has made it her task to self-educate and thus to take control of her disease for the benefit of herself and her son who has HIV. What impressed me most about Violeta's increased involvement in confronting and treating HIV was that she has transitioned from a more passive position, in which she was dependent on case workers and counselors to guide her, to a more active position, in which she relies on her own literacy to read and evaluate treatments. We discussed the fact that she is more actively evaluating her situation by critically reading literature on treating HIV:

> LAUREN: So if you're studying, reading, and writing, and taking care of yourself with your education, then you can get, then you can read and write more—
>
> VIOLETA: More, I can learn about more HIV. I can read in the papers, I can read a paper about medicine, that: "Oh, I'm going to start a new medicine." I know how to read what is going on with this medicine, how this medicine going to work in my body—
>
> L: Is that something that you do?
>
> V: Yeah, before I never do it *porque* I don't know how writing, [*unintelligible*] reading . . . now, step-by-step, that's what I do. They give me the paper in English, and I take it home and I read it about how is this medicine work in the body, learn about more the medicine.

Reading critically allows Violeta to transform herself into an informed patient who can make intelligent decisions for herself and advocate for her own best interest. Her self-advocacy indicates an important change in her subjectivity. In addition to the transition from passively accepting and appreciating the help of others to actively taking charge of her own medical care by reading about her condition, she can discuss medication and treatment more knowledgably with her doctors and counselors.

Violeta's self-advocacy illustrates John Trimbur's point that ordinary people can turn themselves into experts on their own situation. In "Composition and the Circulation of Writing," Trimbur argues that medical journal articles and news reports are parts of a "total system of production" in which they are "joined together in the distribution and authorization of expertise" (213). He refers specifically to how knowledge is disseminated in hierarchized ways as part of a cycle of transferring capital. Those with the greatest medical needs and experience often are silenced by the prominent voices of professional expertise. However, Violeta uses her literacy to read complex medical texts and consult with doctors about her own treatment. This is precisely the kind of resistance that Trimbur recommends. As an informed, well-read patient, Violeta has put herself on a level closer to that of the medical experts. She is able to go to her appointments and meetings and discuss shared knowledge, as she remarks in the following interview excerpt: "I like to go to the meeting and listen to the people when they talking about medicine, or everything. I like to participate a lot. I learn about it, I take free time, I like to workshop [*unintelligible*]. . . . I know more about that." Along with the knowledge Violeta gains as a reader and as a participant in workshops and meetings, she has gained agency as a more literate person who can consult with experts to become her own best advocate.

Throughout the years we have been involved in this research together, Violeta has referred to her dream of becoming a social worker so that she can help others the way people, like her case worker, have helped her. Her desire to eventually become a case manager or social worker is explicitly linked to her ongoing literacy education: "If I finish my school, I want to go to the college and learn. . . ." Her desire is not merely to practice social work, but also to continue to expand her own knowledge. Violeta's career ambition is bound to her desire to continue learning: "I remember when I come to Read/Write/Now, I don't know nothing about English, I don't know this place, and I find good case manager that helping me, *y* that opened the door for me."

Her frequent references to the metaphor of a door being opened show how important literacy education and the support of social service workers and teachers have been to Violeta over the years. Through other people's support and through her own persistence, doors have opened—doors that were previously shut, such as the door to schooling—and Violeta has been able to pass through. Now, she states, "They give it to me, and I want to pass again." Violeta wants to be the person who opens doors for others.[3]

ASSERTING TEXTUAL AGENCY

Creating textual agency means that Chief and Violeta can use the writing process to make several moves they couldn't make previously without writing. They consciously take their writing from private to increasingly public contexts where it can have more of an effect. When Violeta and Chief compose their texts, and when Violeta speaks to new public audiences, they are challenging dominant discourses by offering something else. That something else results from their critique of culture and the affectual urge to communicate what they know to others in public as well as private spheres. By reaching out to take social action—whether that action involves immediate or broader publics—they call attention to a border that is being crossed. They want witnesses to their acts of transgression through writing, and they also desire validation in challenging borders of oppression. They want to call more people to join them in asserting textual agency and in expressing oppositional perspectives.

Yet they are aware of how their words challenge popular narratives. Paula Mathieu and Diana George observe about mainstream news publications a "sameness in coverage that leaves the overall impression that there are no alternative ways to tell these stories" (133). Mathieu and George's dismay over the single perspective that often passes as the news is a good reminder that most of the time we hear only versions of dominant narratives. Stories like Violeta's and Chief's are unusual in that they present alternative stories. Their stories are not only valuable to them for personal action, but they are also valuable to anyone who reads them because we learn about their way of representing the world. When they take the steps to speak out in their writing, they are telling a different story of culture, one that has the potential to change their subjectivity beyond the context of the written narrative.

The circulation of their work is also vital to Violeta and Chief. They want their voices to be heard by others. They do not speak out simply for self-validation and for witnesses to their experiences. The texts themselves matter, and the authors' hope for their texts is that they might—should—be used for social change. As Mathieu and George explain about circulation, "Any changes made or attempted can't be located solely on the page, or in the act of composition, but also are found in the writing's circulation, in how it works in the world, fostering conversation, creating pressure, and even creating unexpected allies" (144). But we may need to reconsider what we mean by circulation and whether this necessarily translates to broad distribution. Violeta's and Chief's experiences with writing suggest that distribution and circulation are not always the same thing, especially when considered from a critical literacy perspective. Their texts circulate differently as a result of their writing even if no one physically sees them—that is, regardless of how extensively they are actually distributed.

Royster and Kirsch coin the term *social circulation* to suggest that ideas can spread more fluidly than we tend to assume. Continuing the feminist argument that rhetorical action is found within traditionally unrecognized acts, they propose that

> [instead] we shift attention more dramatically toward circulations that may have escaped our attention, that we may not have valued (and therefore neglected to study), or that because they are based in women's activities, we may not have immediately envisioned as rhetorical activities. . . . Yet, these kinds of social networks are often civic in nature, rhetorical in function, and both activist and community building in outcome, such that the ideas created within such discourses

have the capacity to compound effects across time and across space. (101)

We see social circulation enacted most explicitly in Violeta's involvement with the public through the production and performance of the DVD. Her work with the community agency that created it has opened up new pathways for her. The writing that Violeta and Chief produce has significant value even when it is circulated in unconventional ways. The routes they take to sharing their texts provide examples of how these writers expose a collision of discourses. We may read their texts expecting that their words will not have a major real-world effect. But, as Royster and Kirsch's concept of "ever-shifting social circles" helps to clarify, although Violeta's and Chief's gestures of circulation appear in previously unsubstantiated forms, it is important for them to share their ideas. It is also important that we follow their example to consider how we might value underrepresented voices differently. Chief demonstrates how he values his own voice when he talks about the importance of distributing his writing about literacy education to members of his sister's church. He believes in the value of his own words, and he also wants people to listen to his words and contemplate them. In this way, he aims to increase and change "public participation" (Trimbur 216) by deliberately using his literacy experience as a model to inspire others to act differently.

When Chief and Violeta circulate their texts, they are attempting to change the way knowledge circulates. They are increasing the range of discourses that can demand our attention. Even when Violeta writes to hypothetical readers, she is already enacting a shift toward new modes of circulation. She did not necessarily need an actual audience to achieve her goals, although she has begun to find them now in her increasingly activist work. Her audiences have shifted, from invoked to actual, demonstrating why, as Royster and Kirsch tell us, we can understand metaphorically the significance of "how ideas resonate, divide, and are expressed via new genres and new media" (101). Violeta's gestures of connecting with audience taught me to acknowledge greater possibilities for what authors might intend, as well as what their texts might achieve.

Trimbur refers to Richard Johnson's use of the term *really use-ful* (Johnson takes it from the *Poor Man's Guardian*) to mean that which is relevant to publics beyond those whose knowledge traditionally counts: "Really useful knowledge, by contrast, would be widely available, circulating throughout the land" (216). But Trimbur explains when he applies Johnson's term: "The crux of really useful knowledge . . . depends in large part on whose questions are taken up" (216). Certainly the authors in this book are not people whose knowledge is generally considered "really useful"; however, when their questions are taken up on their terms, the "crux of really useful knowledge" changes.

Considering this very text in those terms forces us to recognize that Violeta's and Chief's writing has particular value not only for me as a person who was one of their public audiences but also for all potential readers of their texts. In literal terms, they circulated their texts by sharing them with me. As I discuss in Chapters 2 and 3, by sharing their words with me, all four participants were asking that their accounts become circulated among wider networks—to literate audiences (implying white and middle-class readers), to people in higher education, and eventually to the readers of this book.

When they direct their texts toward new, increasingly public audiences, Violeta and Chief exercise their textual agency. Circulation of their texts means the potential to have their voices heard in public contexts. Their gestures of resistance, while usually local and worked out in texts that will possibly be read only by other people like them, still grant them textual agency. As Flynn, Sotirin, and Brady's argument for feminist resilience implies, we do not need to measure the effects of people's work by their success at persuading large audiences. Chief's and Violeta's acts of resistance may seem like small gestures, but given the material conditions they are up against and their internalized sense of having been gazed upon as nonliterate for most of their lives, their moves to confront their positioning and to demonstrate what they have done are significant. They do consciously subvert the culture that has oppressed them when they write; they do deliberately disrupt the domineering discourses while simultaneously learning the conventions that will allow them self-expression through writing. For Violeta and Chief, writing can be a vehicle for contesting the "violence of literacy" (Stuckey; Freire, *Pedagogy*) by offering new public voices that read power differently than dominant models.

The Transgressive Power of Writing

THE DESIRE FOR LITERACY

Not to Be Kept "Hush-Mouth"

IN THE UNITED STATES, THE INABILITY TO read and write is conflated with the inability to speak. To be denied literacy is to be denied a voice, to be kept "hush-mouth," as Chief recalled about his childhood in the segregated South: "[A] lot of that stuff down there was kept hush-mouth." To an extent, Chief is more hopeful than Spivak (who questions whether the subaltern might ever truly speak) because he is focused on himself as an individual who can make changes to his own life. Yet he is also always community minded and conscious of the needs of "the peoples." He is aware of the public gaze, and he has at times internalized the view that "my opinion don't mean nothing here"; it has affected him deeply. Unlike Spivak, Chief does not concern himself with how intellectuals who can count on their voices being heard are going to represent his experience. He does not consider a system in which "the subaltern cannot speak . . . [because] Representation has not withered away" (308).

Spivak's argument, that representation remains a problem even for those who aim to address the issue of colliding discourses, brings me back to my own effort, which has been continually to resist appropriation so that the participants might interpret their own experiences and thus represent themselves. My goal has been to show how the participants claimed their literacy for personal, social, and public purposes, and how strongly they desire to resist, to speak out on the page, and to be acknowledged.

Researchers in education were already concerned with listening to ordinary people's articulation of their lived experience as the basis for creating programs prior to the advent of New Literacy studies and community literacy efforts. As far back as 1979, in their report to the Ford Foundation, *Adult Illiteracy in the United States*, Carman Hunter and David Harman advocated for more federal support for research into the needs of nonliterate Americans from their own perspective. But Hunter and Harman were also wary of the large-scale studies being conducted at the time and of the researchers themselves, observing that "those of us who prepare studies about disadvantaged people run the risk of perpetuating stereotypes. We tend to simplify complex lives into cases to be analyzed, or problems that need solutions, or statistics to be studied" (389). Their remark underscores the necessity of contemplating ordinary people's accounts and allowing their narratives to become the models guiding our research. As Freire tells us about the adult learners he worked with in Brazil,

> I learned there from my relationship with them that I should be humble concerning their wisdom. They taught me by their silence that it was absolutely indispensable for me to put together my knowledge from intellectual study with their own wisdom. . . . They taught me without saying that their language was not inferior to mine[;] . . . they introduced me to the beauty of their language and wisdom, through their witness, their testimony, not through lectures about themselves. (Shor and Freire 29–30)

So, paying careful attention, listening intently, "standing under" their accounts, and asking people what they need and what they want are all critical, whether we work with adults in an informal learning environment or with students in more traditional educational settings. In this way, subaltern voices can be acknowledged as those of authors rather than subordinated others. What matters is that we listen to people and then revise our interpretation to reflect "their witness, their testimony," and to engage in mutual contemplation of their experiences and their writing. Theirs is the "expertise" Flower talks about when she claims that ordinary people can best model the needs of their own communities. If this book makes a contribution to critical literacy studies, it is my hope that it has offered academic researchers in writing studies and education, classroom teachers, ABE workers, and students a lens through which to more clearly understand the lives of adult learners, the reasons why it is vital to them to become more literate, and why what matters to them about writing can also impact us.

I realize now that what I sought when I began to work with adult learners was to understand the "revealing function" Giroux attributes to resistance (qtd. in Chase). I wanted to know how literacy functions for adult learners and how it is different from what formal education tells us is important. What I have found is that in many ways the four authors in this study embrace dominant narratives, craving the rules and standards they believe they missed. But at the same time they seek out the conventions they think they should know to make up for their perceived lack, they engage in an ongoing critique of the system that has oppressed them, and sometimes they actively resist it through their spoken words and their writing.

My impulse is to keep collecting and retelling, contemplating, and circulating stories. But at some point, I, like the learners at Read/Write/Now, have the task of assimilating my experiences into the mainstream culture where we live. The relationships of the participants in this study with their teachers suggest that a particular sense of attunement is essential to their success as literacy learners. Something must be different in their educational experience for people like Lee Ann and Violeta and Chief and George to continue to attend a learning center so persistently. It's not just their urge to seize a moment of their lives and understand that, yes, now is the time to learn differently. Another vital piece is how they are received, the ways in which learners are "read" by teachers, volunteers, their peers at the center, as well as everyone they interact with in the outside world. When there is attunement—moments of connectedness—literacy matters and people are inspired to make important changes in their lives. When they are "kicked to the curb," rejected or ignored or called "dummy," things remain the same, and their voices are hushed.

The idea that subaltern subjects might influence the ways they are gazed upon suggests a change in discourse. Fanon (*Black Skin*) provides the best lens for looking at how adult learners can reconstruct their experiences when they acquire new literacies, and how they can use their literacy to disrupt a Self/Other binary. Countering binaries of oppression does not depend only on the subaltern's resistance. It depends too on people whose experiences have been more privileged (me as a researcher, the readers of this book) also taking up the project of resisting representation of others, of enacting the "withering" of representation that Spivak implies may be possible but still unlikely.

Rupturing the Self/Other Circle

In reflecting on the construction of the Other, Fanon relies on Hegelian philosophy to inform his understanding of how the Self/Other cycle is maintained on both sides of the binary and how the circle of locking another into the position of Other might be ruptured: "The only means of breaking this vicious circle that throws me back on myself is to restore to the other, through mediation and recognition, his human reality, which is different from natural reality" (*Black Skin* 217). It is through their literacy studies that adult learners have opportunities to mediate and recognize in ways different from what they have already known. Though they have been doing this already all their lives through their oral critique, the time and space they provide themselves when they engage in literacy allow them to foreground more introspective actions such as reading, reflecting, restorying, reexamining, and eventually rewriting. This is how the four authors in this book turn the reflective knowledge and wisdom they can already claim to the construction of new knowledge; this is how what they know leads them to know more and to know differently.

Fanon goes on to explain that the process of disrupting the Other starts with awareness of the self:

> In its immediacy, consciousness of self is simple being-for-itself. In order to win the certainty of oneself, the incorporation of the concept of recognition is essential. Similarly, the other is waiting for recognition by us, in order to burgeon into the universal consciousness of self. Each consciousness of self is in quest of absoluteness. (*Black Skin* 217)

Breaking the circle of Self/Other depends on releasing the Other from a position of oppression, a cycle that we all maintain to some extent. Throughout the book, you as readers witness "being-for-itself" in all four of the participants. Violeta, for example, separates herself from the struggles of her life so that she can simply be. For her, *being* clearly represents separation from those who have locked her in (sometimes literally) by deliberately keeping the "door now open." When she talks about the "door now open," and when she writes about possibilities for being for single mothers, she is theorizing how literacy might be turned to personal and social action.

The Self/Other circle can be disrupted when the Other, as a result of his or her explicit gestures of resistance, gains the self-consciousness that allows her to fully experience her desire for literacy. Resistance enables desire. The desire to become more literate is an aspect of resisting the autobiographical script of nonliteracy. Here's how Fanon describes it: "When it encounters resistance from the other, self-consciousness undergoes the experience of *desire*—the first milestone on the road that leads to the dignity of the spirit. Self-consciousness accepts the risk of its life, and consequently it threatens the other in his physical being" (*Black Skin* 218). I don't think it is overly dramatic to say that the four authors were risking their lives in pursuing literacy; I mean that they were risking their lives as they knew them to be. For each of them, becoming more literate meant, at the very least, a shift in perspective, a shift to contemplating texts. They also took the risk of being disgraced, as both George and Lee Ann frequently remarked, of stirring up painful memories, and of being further denigrated by literate oppressors when they confronted the turbulent discourses in their lives and now, specifically, in their literate lives.

For the four authors discussed in this book, the desire for literacy was born of resistance. It is a manifestation of their resistance, rooted in the refusal to remain nonliterate. Their rejection of the subject position of nonliterate constructs their affectual desire and leads to their movement toward literacy, both for its own sake and for the benefits it promises. The desire to become more literate, to engage in literate acts, gave them greater opportunity to restory, to rethink, to be, and to become. These are actions that people can desire and make use of as literate subjects. Their articulation of desire *is* the product of resistance. It is the expression of the wish for something else, to be literate not simply to make up for a lack but also for rich, varied, and multiple meaningful purposes. Resistance initiates their desire. Fanon discusses the relationship of resistance and desire:

> As soon as I *desire* I am asking to be considered. I am not merely here-and-now, sealed into thingness. I am for somewhere else and for something else. I demand that notice be taken of my negating activity insofar as I pursue something other than life; insofar as I do battle for the creation of a human world—that is, of a world of reciprocal recognitions. (*Black Skin* 218)

Chief, Violeta, George, and Lee Ann sought out literacy because it was something they had always wanted. Their affectual desire, above all other factors, inspired them to pursue what they had been denied. Even now in older adulthood, their path toward literacy is sometimes fraught with social and personal obstacles. They show us how people value literacy when it is not taken for granted. When the yearning for literacy is explicit, we can see how it—especially writing—can be used both to accept dominant discourses and to challenge them. We see how the participants continually navigate their roles within social space as they use their newly acquired literacy for personal and social change (Bourdieu, "Social Space"). They are all aware of connections between literacy and acquisition of cultural capital, and their actions reveal just how delicately those connections balance as they actively challenge their position. Their experiences can tell us how literacy can be used to *become* and to *revise*—continuously, critically, and with ongoing personal and social awareness. All four authors know how they have been ideologically positioned throughout their lives, and all have reached a moment when they are prepared to challenge that positioning and alter their autobiographical scripts. Their lived experience has led them to the place they are in now, where they want to interrogate and reflect; all have come to study literacy because they want to make some kind of change.

~

TAKING IT IN AGAIN

As I pull together the pieces of the book, it feels important to return to Read/Write/Now and get back into the mood of the place. I need to verify my perspective. Make certain I got the story right. Be with the people there. Observe and pay attention. Check myself. What do I notice? Do I know what I think I know? I return to italics for this section as once again I stand under the learners at the center for the specific purpose of reflecting on their activity.

Pamela greets me at the door after I knock and wait a few minutes. It is Tuesday, and the main part of the library is closed until 1:00, just before the Read/Write/Now day ends. We sit on a bench in the lobby and talk. First about Melissa. She's been gone from her job for two years now.

None of the participants has died, which was the worry I had returning to the center after a few years away while I was writing this book. As far as Pamela knows, all are well. Lee Ann? Pamela doesn't even remember who she is (this tells me something about research being about a person in a moment). Lee Ann's year-plus stint was short compared to those of the other three, who were deeply involved at Read/Write/Now over a much longer period.

Violeta—was on a waiting list to return to the center. Pamela wrote her a letter when a space opened up but didn't hear back (doesn't know if she got the letter).

George—nothing, but someone said he saw him.

Chief—he's the one who stops in. He is fine. He is still driving that little bus, needs the work. He hasn't had another stroke.

I sit in on the classes and right away I am captivated by the lively personalities of the learners, the warmth and connectedness of a group of people who are in an environment where they want to be, their willingness to take in new experiences. A few of the learners reveal a certain spark or quirk that makes me want to know them.

In the intermediate class, it is vocabulary time. When I join the group, they are reading aloud sentences they wrote that incorporate their vocabulary words.

I'll call him Ralph. Here's his sentence: "My father made a big <u>impact</u> on my life that forced me to go back to school."

Ralph is a white man of about sixty. He has made elaborate sketches in his notebook of raised garden beds that are three to four feet off the ground in wooden boxes. The diagrams are drawn neatly in pencil with measurements written in. I ask Ralph about his drawings, and he explains. The boxes have lattice covers that go over the herbs to protect them so rabbits can't get in. You can have tomato plants too. The drainage goes through there around the edges of the boxes and out one side. Ralph says there's a guy in Vermont or Maine who's making similar boxes, but "these are mines." *He points to a wooden box outside the window in a grassy plot by the parking lot where he's planted garlic for the center.*

There's Calvin, still here since the place opened in 1987, strolling back to join his class. I note a couple of other familiar faces, but in general, this is a different group from the one I used to know.

Another sentence from the vocabulary lesson, this one read aloud by a middle-aged black woman: "I would like to get my CDL license, but at this time, I am a <u>novice</u>." *Before she volunteered to read, this woman leaned toward me to ask where I got my red metallic leather sandals because they match her bronze nail polish (they sort of do). A while later, this woman tells the teacher she has to leave. She can't get her meds right. She just took a Percocet—well, only a piece of a Percocet—and now she needs to leave to wake up. She's going to get into her car and drive home.*

One more compelling interaction: a woman in the class walks behind me with her eyes cast over my shoulder to see what I am writing in my notebook. She says, "Your writing is so pretty. If I could write so pretty, I'd write all the time." *What is this woman implying? I imagine that she sees another woman with a smaller notebook than the kind they use in class and with narrow ruled lines, a woman exhibiting mysteriously fine motor control over the squiggles and lines of words, unlike the lumpy, belabored shapes of the letters she and some of her classmates produce. From a few feet away, she glances at a script that she finds impressive:* "Pretty." *But what is it she wants? To make pretty script? To be able to fill a page of text rapidly? I'd like to think that she wants to write proficiently, that she already has the desire to "write all the time."*

I observe a unique kind of teaching at the literacy center, and maybe it is something we can bring back to our universities. Their position in an informal ABE setting allows the teachers (not Carolyn or Melissa, but new teachers now) flexibility not usually available in more traditional learning environments. Although there is still some need to meet standards (a few state measures they have to comply with to keep their funding), the teachers at Read/Write/Now have little institutional pressure. They can do what they want in terms of designing curricula and determining educational goals along with their students. They can engage in mutual contemplation with their students. They are not preparing learners to get a degree or credential. In this setting with this population, teachers can fully express their compassion. Most of the teaching involves connection: establishing and maintaining trust, acting as a conduit for learning, demonstrating why this work matters and that it can be done. Literacy matters not simply because of what it can get you in terms of economic and cultural capital. It matters, and it is available, not as a set of skills but as a means of knowing and interacting in the world that can be shared. The teachers model it: here's what I've got that I can give to you. The learners are grateful, and the teachers bask in the sense of purpose they gain from their students. One learner states in the new program-wide publication:

[Read/Write/Now] has changed my life forever. And, thank God! I have an amazing teacher who is taking her time for us and answers our questions. I always ask myself how she understands our accents. She never gives up and we never give up. (Read/Write/Now Adult Learning Center, *Writings on Resilience* 28*)*

Literacy learning matters too because of where it takes a person, the learners along with their teachers—to remote parts of the mind and soul that we might not know exist, those places of wandering and rumination that involve the reliving aspects of reading and writing, taking it in and traveling there again. This experience is difficult for a literate person to imagine since so many of us have spent our lives taking for granted the benefits of literacy. As George said in Chapter 3 about China and Russia, when you are nonliterate, you don't even know you can go there because you are not conscious of the mental journey that reading and writing enable.

∼

CONVERSATIONS ON WRITING AND ADULT LEARNERS

Many perspectives have informed and shaped my view of literacy as grounded in affectual desire. Not all nonliterate people share this desire (for that matter, many literate people take their ability for granted and don't regularly consider its value); for those who deliberately seek literacy in adulthood, their urge is particularly complex, as I have suggested. The desire for literacy is distinct from need (does anyone *need* to be literate? probably not). *Why* people want literacy and what it is they want are important. As Anne Ruggles Gere commented in her essay advocating for studies of writing practices outside of schooling, "The extracurriculum I examine is constructed by desire, by the aspirations and imaginations of its participants" (80).

Yet the fields of writing studies and adult basic education don't deal directly enough with the affectual desire for literacy, nor does either discipline explicitly address the writing of adult learners. Scholarship in ABE looks primarily at reading practices and at functional uses of writing, while research in writing studies (including community literacy studies) does not focus extensively on the needs of adult literacy learners. Writing studies still looks most often at the situation of college students despite efforts to be mindful of other populations. Typically we bring our focus back to pedagogy and what to do in college classrooms. We don't look at pedagogy in terms of adult learners. But writing studies scholars can learn from ABE about the needs of populations besides traditional university students, about why and how writing matters. By the same token, ABE can learn from writing studies because ABE doesn't look enough at learners' writing practices other than functional use. It's time for both of these fields to pay attention to the other by looking at where valuable scholarship in each area can inform the other, and by identifying gaps where we can do more work with writing.

Since the New Literacy studies movement popularized research on people's informal reading and writing practices in relation to the discourse of schooling (Street; Gee), there has been a good deal of scholarship in writing studies, education, and adult basic education of "vernacular literacies" (Barton and Hamilton; Farr; Moss, *Literacy*; Purcell-Gates). Various projects in writing studies explore how people relate to literacy in communities outside of formal schooling (Brandt; Cintron; Cushman, "Rhetorician," *Struggle*; Daniell; Gere; Guerra; Herzberg; Moss, *A Community*; Ray), and some focus specifically on the engaged inquiry that defines community literacy (Branch, *Eyes*, "In the Hallways," "What No Literacy"; Flower; Goldblatt, "Alinsky's," *Because*; Grabill; Long; Mathieu; Parks). However, few writing studies scholars have looked at writing composed by adults as they acquire basic literacy later in life. While a number of projects examine the experiences of marginalized populations, such as incarcerated people and other at-risk groups (Branch, *Eyes*; Cintron; Daniell; Jacobi; Mathieu), these don't focus explicitly on the challenges faced by adult learners who may be relating to writing for the first time (Branch's work is an exception).

Linda Brodkey's research on a letter writing exchange between adult learners and their graduate student penpals is one project that delves into the texts produced by developing writers ("On the Subjects of Gender and Class"); however, Brodkey's emphasis is on the disconnects that occur when her middle-class student participants try to engage with people outside their own social class rather than on the literate experiences of their ABE penpals.

Outside of writing studies, particularly in ABE, there is plenty of research on motivations for becoming more literate (Fingeret and Drennon; Gillespie, "Becoming"; Horsman; Rockhill) and on persistence in attending learning programs (Comings; Cuban); yet, as with writing studies, little of this work concentrates primarily on writing by adult learners. While ABE researchers are sensitive to the material realities of learners' lives, much of the scholarship is directed toward securing funding for programs rather than investigating reasons for writing. Programs serving adult students are measured by their ability to bring learners up to GED level, delivering them to the mainstream, and overlooking the conditions that keep some people either removed from the culture of schooling or unable to function within the system when they are placed in it. Generally, funding for adult education depends on assessments of learners that measure "progress," ignoring the mission of some programs like Read/Write/Now that serve learners' individual goals and needs. By perpetuating a deficit model, assessments position adult learners as people who will probably only move up to the bottom of the educational hierarchy, which, our policymakers imply, will be good enough.

The lack of significant research into adult learners' writing practices points to a few problems. The demise of the National Institute for Literacy (NIFL) and the National Center for the Study of Adult Learning and Literacy (NCSALL), the federal programs that supported adult literacy research, reveals that educating struggling American adults is not a priority in this country. Maryland State Director of Adult Education Patricia Bennett reports that "93 million residents in the United States would benefit from adult education and literacy instruction" (vii). National Assessment of Adult Literacy (NAAL) figures and the Maryland State Assessment of Adult Literacy (SAAL) findings suggest that approximately 20 percent of adults in that state struggle to read, write, and compute.

A sizable percentage of the adult population in the United States has difficulty with literacy.

During the last few years that NCSALL was in operation (roughly 2006–2010), their funding was reduced to projects that examined reading skills only (Lopez 13). The predominance of published scholarship on reading, and the general privileging of reading as *the* significant aspect of literacy, reflects a historical pattern. Reading is typically valued as meaningful and pleasurable while writing remains undervalued.

The National Council of Teachers of English (NCTE) has contested this assumption by defining literacy as encompassing "reading, writing, and a variety of social and intellectual practices that call upon the voice as well as the eye and hand. It also extends to new media—including non-digitized multimedia, digitized multimedia, and hypertext or hypermedia" (*Adolescent Literacy* 2). In a 2007 position statement, the organization claimed to value writing as a primary literacy practice, advocating for more classroom prompts "in which students reflect on their current understandings, questions, and learning processes" (3) and for an overall focus on the literacies students use in their everyday lives, including out-of-school reading and writing practices (*Position Statement on Multimodal Literacies* 2, 3). Unsurprisingly, none of the NCTE position statements directly addresses adult literacy (or a concern for the parents/guardians of K–12 students) as a topic for policy research. Despite apparent efforts to prioritize writing, in its concluding recommendations "for policymakers," the policy research brief lists attention to writing as its sixth bullet point and reduces writing to measurable goals: "make sure students attain the skills necessary for effective writing" (*Adolescent Literacy* 6).

The four authors discussed in this book, however, show us that writing is a significant literate act. Rather than ignore or subordinate writing, we should learn from their experiences with literacy that writing has transgressive potential. Even George and Lee Ann, who are not as ready to create texts as Violeta and Chief, still recognize writing as powerful and effective. Especially in Violeta's and Chief's texts, writing provides alternative ways of being and of speaking—speaking out and speaking back to culture.

Despite what we know from the four authors about the transgressive power of writing, most ABE programs do not focus on writing except as a functional skill. Writing has been as underresearched in ABE as it has in public schools. However, though much of the literature in that field concentrates on scores and work-prep skills, some scholarship is concerned with the value of writing for its own sake. For example, in *Literacy for Life*, Hanna Fingeret and Cassandra Drennon interview adult learners who worked with Literacy Volunteers of New York City about their changing relationship to literacy, and to writing specifically, as they went through the program. Fingeret and Drennon's project resembles mine in its focus on the spoken and written accounts of adult learners who attend an innovative program; whereas they analyze their case studies mostly in regard to learners' developing personal agency, I have looked further into the critical agency people gain in the process of acquiring new literacies.

Gillespie's research on adult learners "becoming authors" is the most ambitious work I have seen in ABE. She insists on the need for more studies in adult classrooms that look into the purposes of writing beyond functional use. Gillespie notes that no large-scale studies of writing have been done in ABE, and that much of the existing scholarship on writing in non-school settings is within writing studies. Gillespie's work draws on scholarship in writing studies, which she imports to ABE ("The Forgotten R").

The authors in this study used writing for purposes they didn't have when they were nonliterate. They used writing to interact with culture differently, to contest the subject position of "illiterate," and to deliberately affect others. If we consider writing as offering the possibility for breaking down barriers so that we might connect with Self and Other in ways that disrupt and create, we can understand its possibilities as an act of transgression.

As the four authors in this study have demonstrated repeatedly, people in "marginal settings" (Heller) can become our teachers. When we enter the spaces where they read and write, we can begin to understand other functions of literacy besides gaining academic capital. Understanding the motivations and purposes of learners outside of the academy can help teachers and students to see the many ways people claim agency through literacy. We can learn by considering the perspectives of people in positions that are not traditionally in power.

Writing: The Transgressive Partner of Reading

Much of the writing studies research on literacy theory and practice also assumes "literacy" to mean writing, reading, and increasingly multimodal literacies, which include but are not limited to the digital, as reflected in the *NCTE Definition of 21st-Century Literacies,* NCTE's *Position Statement on Multimodal Literacies,* and the definition in the NCTE policy brief on adolescent literacy (*Adolescent Literacy*) (www.ncte.org/positions/literacy). Although these definitions broaden the notion of literacies to include multiple forms and contexts, the processes of reading, writing, and composing generally remain unquestioned. According to Deborah Brandt's study of people's real-life uses of reading and writing, *Literacy in American Lives,* reading has been privileged historically as the primary literacy skill in the United States while writing has been subordinated. Schools spend more time and money on reading than on writing (163). While the childhood ambition to read often comes from adults or books, Brandt's research shows that writing is less frequently celebrated as an achievement and as a family activity, and that it is often inspired by a sense of aloneness and sadness. Many of the people Brandt interviewed perceived writing as an activity of transgression, associated with venting, withholding, or secretly speaking out, or view it as mundane (paying bills, homework, filling out forms). Memories of writing as painful, difficult, or the cause of trouble remind us why people so often undervalue it.

We have witnessed similar patterns among the people discussed in this book. Lee Ann continues to struggle with writing as a mark of her "inability." When she approaches writing tasks, she wrestles with the details of how to spell and arrange individual words; she becomes frustrated easily as the idea of writing causes her to confront once again painful memories. George reveals that writing has become "a little bit better now." His tendency was to view writing as less important than reading, demonstrating the trend that the literature shows as predominant. However, George's ongoing efforts at writing have taught him to understand its value when he can cast writing as an ordinary act. Then it is less fearsome. Before, he admits, writing seemed like "pressure"; he was "almost afraid to write." We see in George and Lee Ann expressions of the anxiety and sense of danger that is often associated with writing and that maintains it is a subordinate form of literacy.

Writing *is* potentially dangerous. And so reading is celebrated as the safer practice, as George suggests when he remarks that reading may be more important than writing. De Certeau refers to reading as an essentially passive act through which we consume ideology. When we read, we willingly ingest culture. He calls reading "habitable, like a rented apartment" (xxi). Writing, in contrast, demands the deliberation that Violeta and Chief frequently exhibit. Writing is an act of production that renders a person vulnerable to the judgment of readers. People's anxiety about writing, their blocks and sense of themselves as exposed, incorrect, or incapable, occurs in response to the unspoken power of writing. This is especially true for adult learners, who may have been shamed as writers. Lee Ann is a prime example of this shaming. When I think of her as a writer, I cannot help but remember the symbolic marks she used to make on the wall to record her mother's violations of her. The association of writing with transgression (Brandt goes so far as to call it "profane") suggests that writing has the potential to subvert, intervene, expose—in effect, to challenge—power. It is because of its transformative possibilities that people both crave and fear writing. If you write, then you have a voice, and that voice can cause disruption.

Violeta and Chief have looked toward the possibilities of writing to transgress. They welcome opportunities to take on the turbulent flow of conflicting discourses that have oppressed them. As we have seen in both of their work, writing allows them to break free of secrets that have burdened them (the secret of living with HIV, the secret of being kept "illiterate" to maintain a racist system). They deliberately choose writing to counter subordination.

Within schools, writing instruction has been limited in the ways Brandt's research implies, thus restricting its possibilities for activism

(Street). Lack of writing opportunities is "no accident," insists LeCourt ("Beyond the Ludic" 66), echoing Brodkey's argument that schools devalue writing because it lies outside the cycle of intellectual activities that translate into cultural currency (Brodkey, "Writing on the Bias"). If we view school as the main site where an ideology of literacy is disseminated (Street; Rose, *Lives*), then it comes as no surprise that writing is often kicked out of the cycle through which school literacy acts translate into cultural currency.

From the inception of public education, writing instruction has created a moral separation between those who have permission to write and those who do not. Harvey J. Graff, Jenny Cook-Gumperz, and John Trimbur emphasize the influence of a "pan-Protestant morality" on public school curriculum through the eighteenth and nineteenth centuries (Graff, "The Nineteenth-Century" 211). Control of literacy, in terms of who had access to it and for what purposes, could separate citizenry along religious, economic, racial, and professional lines. Writing in particular was discussed in terms of its potential political threat if taught to poor and working-class students. Evangelical educator Hannah More put it this way: "I allow of no writing for the poor. My object is not to make them fanatics, but to train up the lower classes in habits of industry and piety" (qtd. in Trimbur, "Literacy" 289). Underlying such accounts was anxiety about dissent: if the non-ruling classes were given too much writing instruction, they might use it for radical purposes, rising up and demanding change in the social order. This could create a disruption of political and class structures and might also lead to a labor shortage. Limitations placed on writing instruction explain why writing took its place as a secondary literacy skill from the beginning of public education; mass access to writing could enable undesirable opinions to find a public voice.

So writing remains the understudied partner of reading. And adult learners continue to view writing as a mark of their ongoing inability. At times, though, some adult learners are motivated by the urge to resist their positioning. Like Violeta and Chief, they crave opportunities for writing so that they can transgress the boundary of nonliteracy.

Where Do We Go Now?

If we accept the idea of reading as the more passive act of ingesting culture and writing as its more active partner, then the entire concept of what literacy can do shifts. Writing, whether we practice it in formal or informal educational settings or outside of any kind of educational space, can be approached for its transgressive potential. We can turn literacy instruction toward addressing real people's needs, to disrupting the status quo and making changes that benefit people in the communities where they live. I end by considering some of the perspectives within community literacy studies and ABE that potentially come together to attempt this shift, again with an eye toward the crossover of these fields and how that exchange of interests offers possibilities for making the wishes of adult students the center of our focus.

Community literacy scholars take the view that there is potential for a third space where teachers guide their students in navigating between academic and community settings with awareness of the needs and wishes of people in each of these sites. Grabill explains that critical literacy is limited when it abstracts people and institutions instead of focusing on actual spaces of interaction and the transitions between them. Critical literacy should not be the only model for a "'true' empowering literacy" (115); Branch (*Eyes*) warns that in practice it cannot. The interactive setting that Grabill proposes, which recalls Homi Bhabha's third space theory, brings together the functional and the critical in "a literacy that is concerned with *doing* and *moving*" (115, emphasis in original). Within this space, learners' wishes need to be taken just as seriously as critical theory when it is applied in university classrooms (Shor).

Outside of university sanctioned spaces (including community literacy and service learning sites as well as informal learning environments), in ABE programs serving women, Jennifer Horsman similarly advocates for paying greater attention to the perspectives presented by adult learners: "If programs and individual program workers see the participants in their programs as strong, competent adults, rather than 'illiterates' who are other/childlike/silent, they will support women in creating a discourse that contests these images of what it means to have trouble reading and writing" (227–28). Her message, that educators can take a more active and invested stance by listening and questioning dominating discourses alongside learners, can be easily extended to an audience of all educators who work with marginalized populations, and especially to writing studies specialists concerned with how students make meaning through their writing. The challenge is not to accommodate conditions as they are (which a discourse of "overcoming" adversity tends to do—looking at an individual's problems as an obstacle to finding wholeness as a citizen), but to work with our students in locating spaces of contradiction and resistance, both in what they read and in what they produce when they write.

As a now longtime reader of adult learners' narratives, I learn from these authors to examine carefully what and why I teach, at whose advantage, and at whose expense. I want their stories to keep telling tell me something about what it means to be a literate individual. If we understand writing as a transgressive act that has the potential both to cause and to harness a turbulent flow of discourse, then we can understand how writing can be seen as threatening or as empowering depending on its use, depending on what it might achieve and who might benefit or suffer as a consequence. The ways that writing is avoided and feared (Brandt) can remind us of its transgressive potential and of why its accessibility is so important for all people, for all voices, to be heard.

⁓

A LAST LOOK

Another visit to Read/Write/Now on publication day: This year's "book" is called Writings on Resilience. *The teachers unpack it from the box and pass out copies. Every learner has made a contribution. The pieces range from poems to essays, and all of them are autobiographical, with a focus on facing personal struggle. Many are untitled and some are anonymously authored. A few of the learners have printed out a separate copy of the piece they intend to read. They handle the pages on the table; their frenetic movements to arrange and rearrange the paper* reveal that they are clearly preoccupied by the prospect of reading their work.

My daughter, just back from her first year of college and who has expressed minimal interest in my research until now, has accompanied me. I watch her take in the black, brown, and white faces around the library tables; the Western and African clothing; the sandaled feet of Caribbean men; the younger and older learners. All three classes are gathered for the reading. A few of the people I met at my last visit shout their greetings across the room. They ask my daughter's name. "How's your book?" calls Ralph, even though it has been only two weeks since we first spoke and I told his class about this book project.

I take out my notebook and pen but not for long. Pamela walks over and whispers to me: Some people said they don't want you taking notes. Is it okay for you not to write? Of course it's fine. I slip my notebook and pen into my bag, sure that whoever voiced the complaint is watching. I am embarrassed by my insensitivity, my assumption that I have carte blanche to take out my notebook anywhere without posing a threat. Did I used to be more aware of things like this? I should have been better able to predict that people might view a writer as a reporter or evaluator who is going to document and expose them. And really, while people read aloud, and we all follow along in the publication, there is no time for writing.

I take in the tension and the pleasure at the reading. People stand up and read their own narratives. They read a classmate's. They read with a teacher at their side helping to get the words right. One man starts to read, and after the first sentence about the dissolution of his marriage, he breaks down sobbing. His teacher finishes for him. Afterwards, he leaves the library with something of a smile and less stress in his eyes, content perhaps that the words are out in public.

A white man with a narrow, wrinkly red throat, gritty voice, and black cap with veterans' pins on it approaches my daughter and me as we exit the library. "I couldn't do it," he announces, but then he tells us the page in the publication where we can find his narrative, and he watches me read the text to myself. "It's hard," he says, meaning hard to read aloud at the presentation with his classmates; then his remarks about reading aloud shift into an explanation of the piece he contributed to the publication, his connection with his own daughter, whom he didn't see for more than twenty years. His story leaks out: moving up north from New Orleans so he can see his daughter, struggling as a veteran, and now his wish both to learn here at the center and to start a business. He's in the glass business, and by that he means beveled glass, the kind that's cut to fit into windows and doors, and stained glass for churches. "It's not that hard," he says, and you don't need a lot. You can tell that he's thought through his ambition for a while and that he's got a plan for how to outfit a van and where to load the glass, as well as which Internet sources to use for sending blueprints and getting the glass cut and sent back to him. His plan is elaborate, and it's wound together with his other intention, to keep coming back to the center after the summer break (it has been only three months since he started) to learn more, partly to become a better businessman but also because "this" [literacy] is something he is sure he needs.

"The people are so motivated," my daughter remarks repeatedly during the car ride home, comparing the learners at Read/Write/Now with students at her college who bemoan their workload and the time of their morning classes, and with high school students who just plain hate it. She has been questioning the motivations of these mainstream students—her peers—and this visit has given her focus and left her with a different lens for that inquiry.

~

NOTES

1. Resisting Nonliteracy: Adult Learners Restory Their Narratives

1. I use the term *nonliterate* to name people who have not had the benefit of becoming literate and *nonliteracy* to name the condition of not knowing how to read or write. When I use the more common "illiterate" and "illiteracy," I am referring to labels that are socially imposed. Therefore, I will always use these words in quotes to call attention to the way "illiteracy" is constructed as a social *illness*. When "illiteracy" is cast as pathological, the term can be used to blame individuals for a slew of social problems. Mike Rose too calls "illiteracy" "a problematic term. I suppose that academics use it because it is rhetorically effective (evoking the specter of illiteracy to an audience of peers, legislators, or taxpayers can be awfully persuasive) or because it is emotionally satisfying" ("Language" 354).

2. When I write about "people," I am generalizing, but not about all people. In identifying "the *politics* of the people," Gayatri Chakravorty Spivak refers to Ranajit Guha's stratification grid for colonial social production. Guha uses the terms *people* and *subaltern classes* synonymously (Spivak 284). I am naming a particular population in a similar way, using *people* to refer to those "defined as a difference from the elite" (285).

3. Spivak's original intent in "Can the Subaltern Speak?" was to challenge Gilles Deleuze's remarks about representation of oppressed groups. In "Intellectuals and Power: A Conversation between Michel Foucault and Gilles Deleuze," Deleuze observes of Foucault's work on prisoners that "a theorising intellectual, for us, is no longer a subject, a representing or representative consciousness. Those who act and struggle are no longer represented, either by a group or a union that appropriates the right to stand as their conscience. Who speaks and acts? It is always a multiplicity, even within the person

who speaks and acts" (206). Spivak takes issue with the "immense problems" implicit in Deleuze's comment by respinning the question of how to represent "those who act and struggle" as a critique of First World postmodern intellectuals (275).

4. Fanon writes about the effects of colonialism as an "important mental pathology which is the direct product of oppression" (*Wretched* 251). Similarly, I see nonliteracy as pathological to the extent that it becomes internalized by those oppressed by it. That pathology is not a condition of the individual (the "illiterate"); rather, it is symptomatic of a range of social problems that are acted out on some individuals.

5. The problem of representation is delicate. If I didn't write the stories of the four people in this book, they would never document them themselves. I don't claim that out of any kind of pleasure over my own power. Outside of an academic community—or a public one interested in showcasing people's stories (such as National Public Radio's StoryCorps)—there are few opportunities for adult learners to put their stories into writing and to be heard publicly (beyond their literacy center and maybe among family and friends). Representation still (and maybe always) remains a problem, even as I argue that I'm trying to do it differently.

6. Linda Flower makes the related assertion that it is the responsibility of academic researchers who are invested in community literacy work to recognize when "expertise comes in unfamiliar discourse packages" (55).

7. Because Kung Suk acts out of her own "free will" when she pursues literacy and when she denigrates herself (neither literacy nor its absence is imposed on her), her pattern is confusing. Althusser explains that we maintain Ideological State Apparatuses in this way, through our belief that our choices are our own (125).

8. F. Michael Connelly and D. Jean Clandinin explain that "in an inductive mode, data more clearly tell their own story" (11). For each person, I coded the first interview transcripts for expressions of their motivations for seeking literacy; I also coded the texts for expressions of their purposes for writing. I marked passages that stood out because the writer seemed to be saying something different,

perhaps something that retold an experience in different language or a different form from ones they had used previously. I searched for passages in which participants might be expressing something that challenged dominant discourse or suggested what might be an alternative discourse, and I marked those to develop into questions for the second interviews. Participants' spoken narratives about their literacy histories provided a context for me to read their stories in terms of each person's lived experience. I used a similar coding system in the second interviews to mark motivations for seeking literacy and purposes for writing. While the themes expressed verbally in interviews were not necessarily the same ones I picked out in writing, the two sets of themes informed each other. In general, the interviews gave me information about each person's lived experience and his or her relationship to literacy in the past and present. The interviews gave me a sense of how each participant positioned him- or herself in relation to writing, whereas the texts revealed how each person was actually using writing.

9. When I conducted the first two interviews with Violeta and Chief, neither could answer the question "How do you define *literacy*?" I was surprised by their unfamiliarity with the term. So, for the third and fourth interviews (George, Lee Ann), I added two questions about *literacy* and *illiteracy*: 1. Are the words *literacy* and *illiteracy* familiar to you? 2. Can you define the term *illiteracy*? George and Lee Ann were able to define *illiteracy* but were less clear about the meaning of *literacy*. In defining both terms, learners did not use the word *literacy* to describe themselves or their learning. Chief and Violeta's incomprehension suggests that the term *literacy* is used by the academic community but not by learners themselves.

10. Whereas the first interviews all took place at Read/Write/Now, most of the second interviews occurred at participants' kitchen tables. There we had lots of room to spread out copies of their portfolios and notebooks, as well as my recording equipment. I also wanted a more intimate space that allowed the participants and me to probe their texts and transcripts together. Only George requested that we meet at the learning center rather than at his home.

11. As opposed to "dropping out," adult learners who leave their programs are said to be "stopping out," the assumption being that they are taking a break to tend to the demands of their lives (Comings).

When they return to their programs, they "stop back in." Thus, the stigma of having dropped out, or failed again, is lifted. Conditions in their lives that may make it necessary for them to leave the program become contextualized as life events rather than indications that one is not a serious enough student to become fully literate.

2. Speaking from "the Silent, Silenced Center": "Just Because You Can't Read Doesn't Mean That You Don't Know"

1. In a few exceptions, I include a brief quote from a participant within one of my italicized passages.

2. Massachusetts offers a nonwritten test, which has made it possible for many of the learners at Read/Write/Now to obtain a license. For some people, the desire to read road signs is one of their primary motivations for coming to the center. George and Chief both talked about always wanting to read the signs on the road when they traveled as a reason for learning to read.

3. The *violence of literacy* is a term coined by J. Elspeth Stuckey, who argues that literacy is sometimes used as a weapon by literate people to wield power over those who are less literate. Lee Ann's narrative certainly makes it clear how literacy can become a means for ostracizing and thus maintaining a segregated society.

3. Contemplating Literacy: "A Door Now Open"

1. The "About Us" introduction to the center's twentieth anniversary anthology characterizes the program as follows: "Read/Write/Now is still one of the few programs in the city that offers basic literacy classes. . . . Reading and writing are afforded equal time in our classes, and publishing student writing is an important part of the program."

2. The "intermediate" class is the highest level at Read/Write/Now. Chief and George both started in the "developing" group but were in the intermediate "pre-GED" class during the time I knew them.

3. "Opening the door" is a recurring theme of Violeta's that I touch on throughout these chapters and in an article in *The Community Literacy Journal*, "'You Have to Knock at the Door for the Door Get Open': Alternative Literacy Narratives and the Development of Textual Agency in Writing by Newly Literate Adults."

4. In an article in *Reflections*, I look into the ways George evaluates his sense of himself performing the autobiographical script of the "illiterate." He imagines a scenario in which he and I appear before a judge: "Quite naturally you are going to plead your case twice time better than I plead mine. Thing is I might wants to say, and I might, you know; but I don't know how to put it in the proper word or—. So, the judge ain't going to listen. . . . I [can't] speak the word that I don't know." His remarks highlight his critical awareness of how the testimony of a person with "the proper word" is privileged over that of one who doesn't "know" ("Retelling Culture" 78).

5. Threaded through all of my notes on George, I find comments to myself like this one: "I am trying to get George to articulate motivations that do not necessarily link to work."

6. Notice that I use the word *story* to refer to participants' transcripts and to their written narratives. I chose this word in an effort not to complicate their interpretation by imposing terms from my research process.

7. Seidman comments that "the narratives we shape of the participants we have interviewed are necessarily limited. Their lives go on; our presentations of them are framed and reified" (111). The life captured in an interview (or even throughout a research study) is just about moments of interaction between researcher and participant, interviewer and interviewee.

4. Literacy and Nonliteracy: Reflective Knowledge and Critical Consciousness

1. I assume that "Taking Off the Masks" was the first piece Violeta wrote on masks because it uses the format that Read/Write/Now teachers recommended and because it presents topics in her life with less analysis than in "My Mask." Unfortunately, we did not discuss the order in which the poems were written. During the time of my research, the publication had not yet come out, and I was not aware that Violeta had composed "Taking Off the Masks" until a later phase of my analysis. I would have liked to talk with her about the composition of both pieces.

2. During this unit, learners were involved in a papier-mâché mask-making project in conjunction with the writing they were doing on

"the masks we wear." The narratives written for this unit eventually constituted a publication with the same title.

3. Chief's quartet group stands in stark contrast to Lee Ann's church choir, where literacy was used to exclude certain members. In Chief's singing group, being a good lyricist does not depend on being literate. If someone writes a song, everyone in the group can be expected to learn it through memorization. Chief's example highlights the inclusiveness of a singing group in which music is learned orally. One does not need to be literate to participate.

5. What Writing Enables

1. Elbow makes a similar claim about a subject's relationship to speech versus writing in "The Shifting Relationships between Speech and Writing."

2. My research with Violeta centered on discussions of the DVD, which I was able to watch and analyze because the filmmakers permitted me to have a copy. Our subsequent interview was about the DVD and her involvement in the project. Although I have transcribed and translated the recording, my IRB prohibits me from sharing images. I have decided not to include the transcript or my interpretations of the text here for ethical reasons. In the future, I hope to do more analysis of Violeta's ongoing development of new literacies.

3. Around the time that we were working on the interview, Violeta told me that her son's case manager had asked if she would be interested in working at Bay State Hospital as a lay counselor. She would meet other people who have HIV and advise them about living with the disease. Violeta told the caseworker that she would think about it but that she might not be ready to go to work yet. She explained to me that she still wants to work on her speaking, reading, and writing skills. She doesn't yet think that her English is good enough to enter the workplace.

WORKS CITED

Ahmed, Sara. *The Cultural Politics of Emotion*. New York: Routledge, 2004. Print.

Althusser, Louis. *On the Reproduction of Capitalism: Ideology and Ideological State Apparatuses*. Trans. G. M. Goshgarian. London: Verso, 2014. Web. 27 July 2014.

Barton, David, and Mary Hamilton. *Local Literacies: Reading and Writing in One Community*. London: Routledge, 1998. Print.

Bennett, Patricia, Foreword. Comings, Garner, and Smith vii–x.

Biesecker, Barbara A. "Rethinking the Rhetorical Situation from within the Thematic of *Différance*." *Philosophy and Rhetoric* 22.2 (1989): 110–30. Print.

Bourdieu, Pierre. *Distinction: A Social Critique of the Judgement of Taste*. Trans. Richard Nice. Cambridge: Harvard UP, 1984. Print.

———. "Social Space and Symbolic Power." *Sociological Theory* 7.1 (1989): 14–25. Print.

Branch, Kirk. *Eyes on the Ought to Be: What We Teach about When We Teach about Literacy*. Cresskill: Hampton, 2007. Print.

———. "In the Hallways of the Literacy Narrative: Violence and the Power of Literacy." *Multiple Literacies for the 21st Century*. Ed. Brian Huot, Beth Stroble, and Charles Bazerman. Cresskill: Hampton, 2004. 15–38. Print.

———. "What No Literacy Means: Literacy Events in the Absence of Literacy." *Reflections: Writing, Service-Learning, and Community Literacy*. 9.3 (2010): 52–74. Print.

Brandt, Deborah. *Literacy in American Lives*. Cambridge: Cambridge UP, 2001. Print.

Britton, James. *Language and Learning: The Importance of Speech in Children's Development*. 2nd ed. Portsmouth: Boynton/Cook, 1993. Print.

Brodkey, Linda. "On the Subjects of Class and Gender in 'The Literacy Letters.'" *College English* 51.2 (1989): 125–41. Print.

———. "Writing on the Bias." *Writing Permitted in Designated Areas Only.* Minneapolis: U Minnesota P, 1996. 30–51. Print.

Charmaz, Kathy. *Constructing Grounded Theory: A Practical Guide through Qualitative Analysis.* London: Sage, 2006. Print.

Chase, Geoffrey, "Accommodation, Resistance and the Politics of Student Writing." *College Composition and Communication* 39.1 (1988): 13–22. Print.

Cintron, Ralph. *Angels' Town: Chero Ways, Gang Life, and Rhetorics of the Everyday.* Boston: Beacon, 1997. Print.

Comings, John P. "Persistence: Helping Adult Education Students Reach Their Goals." Comings, Garner, and Smith 23–46.

Comings, John P., Barbara Garner, and Cristine Smith, eds. *Review of Adult Learning and Literacy: Connecting Research, Policy, and Practice.* Vol. 7. Mahwah: Erlbaum, 2007. Print.

Connelly, F. Michael, and D. Jean Clandinin. "Stories of Experience and Narrative Inquiry." *Educational Researcher* 19.5 (1990): 2–14. Print.

Cook-Gumperz, Jenny. "Literacy and Schooling: An Unchanging Equation?" *The Social Construction of Literacy.* Ed. Jenny Cook-Gumperz. Cambridge: Cambridge UP, 1986. 16–44. Print.

Cuban, Sondra, "'So Lucky to Be Like That, Somebody Care:' Two Case Studies of Women Learners and Their Persistence in a Hawai'i Literacy Program." *Adult Basic Education* 13.1 (2003): 19–43. Print.

Cushman, Ellen. "The Rhetorician as an Agent of Social Change." *College Composition and Communication* 47.1 (1996): 7–28. Print.

———. *The Struggle and the Tools: Oral and Literate Strategies in an Inner City Community.* Albany: State U of New York P, 1998. Print.

Cushman, Ellen, Eugene R. Kintgen, Barry M. Kroll, and Mike Rose, eds. *Literacy: A Critical Sourcebook.* Boston: Bedford/St. Martin's, 2001 Print.

Daniell, Beth. *A Communion of Friendship: Literacy, Spiritual Practice, and Women in Recovery.* Urbana: NCTE/CCCC; Carbondale: Southern Illinois UP, 2003. Print.

Dean, Thomas, Barbara Roswell, and Adrian J. Wurr, eds. *Writing and Community Engagement: A Critical Sourcebook.* Boston: Bedford/St. Martin's, 2010. Print.

De Certeau, Michel. *The Practice of Everyday Life.* Trans. Steven Rendall. Berkeley: U of California P, 1984. Print.

Elbow, Peter. "Reflections on Academic Discourse: How It Relates to Freshmen and Colleagues." *College English* 53.2 (1991): 135–55. Print.

———. "The Shifting Relationships between Speech and Writing." *College Composition and Communication* 36.3 (1985): 283–303. Print.

———. "Writing and Magic." *Writing with Power: Techniques for Mastering the Writing Process.* 2nd ed. New York: Oxford UP, 1998. 357–73. Print.

Fanon, Frantz. *Black Skin, White Masks.* Trans. Charles Lam Markmann. New York: Grove, 1967. Print.

———. *The Wretched of the Earth.* Trans. Constance Farrington. New York: Grove, 1963. Print.

Farr, Marcia, ed. *Ethnolinguistic Chicago: Language and Literacy in the City's Neighborhoods.* Mahwah: Erlbaum, 2004. Print.

Fingeret, Hanna Arlene, and Cassandra Drennon. *Literacy for Life: Adult Learners, New Practices.* New York: Teachers College P, 1997. Print.

Flower, Linda. *Community Literacy and the Rhetoric of Public Engagement.* Carbondale: Southern Illinois UP, 2008. Print.

Flynn, Elizabeth, Patricia Sotirin, and Ann Brady, eds. *Feminist Rhetorical Resilience: Possibilities and Impossibilities.* Logan: Utah State UP, 2012. Print.

Foucault, Michel. "The Ethic of Care for the Self as a Practice of Freedom." *The Final Foucault.* Ed. James Bernauer and David Rasmussen. Cambridge: MIT P, 1987. 1–21. Print.

———. "The Subject and the Power." Afterword. *Michel Foucault: Beyond Structuralism and Hermeneutics.* Ed. Hubert L. Dreyfus and Paul Rabinow. Chicago: U of Chicago P, 1982. 208–29. Print.

Foucault, Michel, and Gilles Deleuze. "Intellectuals and Power: A Conversation between Michel Foucault and Gilles Deleuze." *Language, Counter-Memory, Practice: Selected Essays and Interviews* by Michel Foucault. Ed. Donald F. Bouchard. Trans. Donald F. Bouchard and Sherry Simon. Ithaca: Cornell UP, 1977. 205–17. Print.

Freeman, Mark. *Rewriting the Self: History, Memory, Narrative.* London: Routledge, 1993. Print.

Freire, Paulo. "The Adult Literacy Process as a Cultural Action for Freedom" and "Education and Conscientização." Cushman, Kintgen, Kroll, and Rose 616–28.

———. *Pedagogy of the Oppressed.* 1970. New York: Continuum, 1993. Print.

Gee, James Paul. "'Literacy, Discourse and Linguistics: Introduction' and 'What Is Literacy?'" Cushman, Kintgen, Kroll, and Rose 525–44.

George, Diana. "The Word on the Street: Public Discourse in a Culture of Disconnect." Deans, Roswell, and Wurr 50–60.

Gere, Anne Ruggles. "Kitchen Tables and Rented Rooms: The Extracurriculum of Composition." *College Composition and Communication* 45.1 (1994): 75–92. Print.

Gillespie, Marilyn K. "Becoming Authors: The Social Context of Writing and Local Publishing by Adult Beginning Readers." Diss. U of Massachusetts, 1991. Print.

———. "The Forgotten R: Why Adult Educators Should Care about Writing Instruction." Twentieth Annual Rutgers Invitational Symposium on Education (RISE). Rutgers University, New Brunswick. 23–24 Oct. 2003. Address.

Giroux, Henry A. *Border Crossings: Cultural Workers and the Politics of Education.* New York: Routledge, 1992. Print.

———. "Literacy and the Politics of Difference." *Critical Literacy: Politics, Praxis, and the Postmodern.* Ed. Colin Lankshear and Peter L. McLaren. Albany: State U of New York P, 1993. 367–77. Print.

Goldblatt, Eli. "Alinsky's Reveille: A Community-Organizing Model of Neighborhood-Based Literacy Projects." *College English* 67.3 (2005): 274–94. Print.

———. *Because We Live Here: Sponsoring Literacy Beyond the Curriculum.* Cresskill: Hampton, 2007. Print.

Grabill, Jeffrey T. *Community Literacy Programs and the Politics of Change.* Albany: State U of New York P, 2001. Print.

Graff, Harvey J. *The Literacy Myth: Literacy and Social Structure in the Nineteenth-Century City.* New York: Academic, 1979. Print.

———. "The Nineteenth-Century Origins of Our Times." Cushman, Kintgen, Kroll, and Rose 211–33.

Gramsci, Antonio. *Selections from* The Prison Notebooks. Ed. and Trans. Quintin Hoare and Geoffrey Nowell Smith. New York: International, 1971. Print.

Guerra, Juan C. *Close to Home: Oral and Literate Practices in a Transnational Mexicano Community.* New York: Teachers College P, 1998. Print.

Heath, Shirley Brice. *Ways with Words: Language, Life, and Work in Communities and Classrooms.* Cambridge: Cambridge UP, 1983. Print.

Heller, Caroline E. *Until We Are Strong Together: Women Writers in the Tenderloin.* New York: Teachers College P, 1997. Print.

Herrington, Anne J. "Gone Fishin': Rendering and the Uses of Personal Experience in Writing." *Writing with Elbow.* Ed. Pat Belanoff, Marcia Dickson, Sheryl I. Fontaine, and Charles Moran. Logan: Utah State UP, 2002. Print. 223–238.

Herzberg, Bruce. "Community Service and Critical Teaching." *College Composition and Communication* 45.3 (1994): 307–19. Print.

Hesford, Wendy S. *Framing Identities: Autobiography and the Politics of Pedagogy.* Minneapolis: U of Minnesota P, 1999. Print.

Horning, Alice. "The History and Role of Libraries in Adult Literacy." *Community Literacy Journal* 5.1 (2010): 151–72. Print.

Horsman, Jennifer. *Something in My Mind Besides the Everyday: Women and Literacy.* Toronto: Women's, 1990. Print.

Hunter, Carman St. John, and David Harman. "Who Are the Adult Illiterates?" *Adult Illiteracy in the United States: A Report to the Ford Foundation.* New York: McGraw, 1979. Rpt. in *Perspectives on Literacy.* Ed. Eugene R. Kintgen, Barry M. Kroll, and Mike Rose. Carbondale: Southern Illinois UP, 1988. 378–90. Print.

Jacobi, Tobi. "Slipping Pages through Razor Wire: Literacy Action Projects in Jail." *Community Literacy Journal* 2.2 (2008): 67–86. Print.

Johnson, T. R. *A Rhetoric of Pleasure: Prose Style and Today's Composition Classroom.* Portsmouth: Boynton/Cook, 2003. Print.

LeCourt, Donna. "Beyond the Ludic: The Materiality of Text Production—A Response to Peter McLaren." *Strategies: Journal of Theory, Culture, and Politics* 11/12 (1998): 56–68. Print.

———. *Identity Matters: Schooling the Student Body in Academic Discourse.* Albany: State U of New York P, 2004. Print.

Long, Elenore. *Community Literacy and the Rhetoric of Local Publics.* Anderson: Parlor, 2008. Print.

Lopez, Noreen. "The Years 2004 and 2005 in Review." Comings, Garner, and Smith 1–22.

Mahala, Daniel, and Jody Swilky. "Telling Stories, Speaking Personally: Reconsidering the Place of Lived Experience in Composition." *JAC* 16.3 (1996): 363–88. Print.

Mathieu, Paula. *Tactics of Hope: The Public Turn in English Composition.* Portsmouth: Boynton/Cook, 2005. Print.

Mathieu, Paula, and Diana George. "*Not* Going It Alone: Public Writing, Independent Media, and the Circulation of Homeless Advocacy." *College Composition and Communication* 61.1 (2009): 130–49. Print.

McLaren, Peter. *Critical Pedagogy and Predatory Culture: Oppositional Politics in a Postmodern Era.* London: Routledge, 1995. Print.

Moss, Beverly J. *A Community Text Arises: A Literate Text and a Literacy Tradition in African-American Churches.* Cresskill: Hampton, 2003. Print.

———, ed. *Literacy across Communities.* Cresskill: Hampton, 1994. Print.

National Council of Teachers of English. *Adolescent Literacy: A Policy Research Brief.* Urbana: NCTE, 2007. Web. 27 July 2014.

———. *The NCTE Definition of 21st-Century Literacies.* Urbana: NCTE, 2013. Web. 28 July 2014.

———. *Position Statement on Multimodal Literacies.* Urbana: NCTE, 2005. Web. 28 July 2014.

Parks, Stephen. *Gravyland: Writing Beyond the Curriculum in the City of Brotherly Love.* Syracuse: Syracuse UP, 2010. Print.

Purcell-Gates, Victoria, "A World without Print." Cushman, Kintgen, Kroll, and Rose 402–17.

———, ed. *Cultural Practices of Literacy: Case Studies of Language, Literacy, Social Practice, and Power.* Mahwah: Erlbaum, 2007. Print.

Ratcliffe, Krista. *Rhetorical Listening: Identification, Gender, Whiteness.* Carbondale: Southern Illinois UP, 2005. Print.

Ray, Ruth E. *Beyond Nostalgia: Aging and Life-Story Writing.* Charlottesville: UP of Virginia. 2000. Print.

Read/Write/Now Adult Learning Center. *My Life So Far . . . : An Anthology by the Learners at the Read/Write/Now Adult Learning Center.* Springfield: Read/Write/Now Adult Learning Center, 2008. Print.

———. *Writings on Resilience: By Adult Learners at the Read/Write/Now Adult Learning Center.* Springfield: Read/Write/Now Adult Learning Center, 2013. Print.

Rockhill, Kathleen. "Gender, Language and the Politics of Literacy." *British Journal of Sociology of Education* 8.2 (1987): 153–67. Print.

Rose, Mike. "The Language of Exclusion: Writing Instruction at the University." *College English* 47.4 (1985): 341–59. Print.

———. *Lives on the Boundary: A Moving Account of the Struggles and Achievements of America's Educationally Underprepared.* New York: Penguin, 1989. Print.

Rosenberg, Lauren. "Retelling Culture through the Construction of Alternative Literacy Narratives: A Study of Adults Acquiring New Literacies. *Reflections: Writing, Service-Learning, and Community Literacy* 9.3 (2010): 75–114. Print.

———. "'You Have to Knock at the Door for the Door Get Open': Alternative Literacy Narratives and the Development of Textual Agency in Writing by Newly Literate Adults." *Community Literacy Journal* 2.2 (2008): 113–44. Print.

Rosenberg, Lauren, and Kirk Branch. "A Conversation about Literacy Narratives and Social Power." *Reflections: Writing, Service-Learning, and Community Literacy* 9.3 (2010): 115–28. Print.

Rousculp, Tiffany. "When the Community Writes: Re-Envisioning the SLCC DiverseCity Writing Series." Deans, Roswell, and Wurr 386–400. Print.

Royster, Jacqueline Jones. "When the First Voice You Hear Is Not Your Own." *College Composition and Communication* 47.1 (1996): 29–40. Print.

Royster, Jacqueline Jones, and Gesa E. Kirsch. *Feminist Rhetorical Practices: New Horizons for Rhetoric, Composition, and Literacy Studies.* Carbondale: Southern Illinois UP, 2012. Print.

Seidman, Irving. *Interviewing as Qualitative Research: A Guide for Researchers in Education and the Social Sciences.* 2nd ed. New York: Teachers College P, 1998. Print.

Shor, Ira. "What Is Critical Literacy?" *Critical Literacy in Action: Writing Words, Changing Worlds.* Ed. Ira Shor and Caroline Pari. Portsmouth: Boynton/Cook, 1999. 1–30. Print.

Shor, Ira, and Paulo Freire, *A Pedagogy for Liberation: Dialogues on Transforming Education.* Westport: Bergin, 1987. Print.

Sohn, Katherine Kelleher. *Whistlin' and Crowin' Women of Appalachia: Literacy Practices since College.* Urbana: NCTE/CCCC; Carbondale: Southern Illinois UP, 2006. Print.

Spivak, Gayatri Chakravorty. "Can the Subaltern Speak?" *Marxism and the Interpretation of Culture.* Ed. Cary Nelson and Lawrence Grossberg. Urbana: U of Illinois P, 1988. 271–313. Print.

Street, Brian V. *Literacy in Theory and Practice.* Cambridge: Cambridge UP, 1984. Print.

Stuckey, J. Elspeth. *The Violence of Literacy.* Portsmouth: Boynton/Cook, 1991. Print.

Sullivan, Patricia A. "Ethnography and the Problem of the 'Other.'" *Ethics and Representation in Qualitative Studies of Literacy.* Ed. Peter Mortensen and Gesa E. Kirsch. Urbana: NCTE, 1996. 97–114. Print.

Trimbur, John. "Composition and the Circulation of Writing." *College Composition and Communication* 52.2 (2000): 188–219. Print.

———. "Literacy and the Discourse of Crisis." *The Politics of Writing Instruction: Postsecondary.* Ed. Richard Bullock and John Trimbur. Portsmouth: Boynton/Cook, 1991. 277–95. Print.

Villanueva, Victor. "*Memoria* Is a Friend of Ours: On the Discourse of Color." *College English* 67.1 (2004): 9–19. Print.

Winterowd, W. Ross. *Senior Citizens Writing: A Workshop and Anthology, with an Introduction and Guide for Workshop Leaders.* West Lafayette: Parlor, 2007. Print.

INDEX

AUTHOR

Lauren Rosenberg is an associate professor of English at Eastern Connecticut State University. She regularly teaches first-year writing courses as well as courses in community literacy, composition theory, and creative writing; until recently she coordinated the first-year writing program. Her writing has appeared in *Community Literacy Journal*; *Reflections: Writing, Service-Learning, and Community Literacy*; and in a number of coauthored book chapters and articles on feminist rhetorical practices and writing program administration. Threaded through all of Rosenberg's work is a commitment to examining and advocating for equity through community engagement and public activism. Her early work in service learning and composition with newly arrived immigrant groups led to a career-long interest in the literacy practices of underrepresented populations. Rosenberg's literacy research extends from the study of adult learners that became this book into a new project that looks into the discourses of writing practiced by military veterans while in service in relation to those they develop as university students. She lives in western Massachusetts.

OTHER BOOKS IN THE CCCC STUDIES IN WRITING & RHETORIC SERIES

This book was typeset in Garamond and Frutiger by Barbara Frazier.
Typefaces used on the cover include Adobe Garamond and Formata.
The book was printed on 55-lb. Natural Offset paper
by King Printing Company, Inc.